THE HISTORICAL ASSOCIATION
BOOK OF

THE TUDORS

The Historical Association
book of

THE
TUDORS

Edited by Joel Hurstfield

SIDGWICK & JACKSON
LONDON

I.S.B.N. 0.283.97874.0

*Printed in Great Britain by
The Garden City Press Limited
Letchworth, Hertfordshire SG6 1JS
for Sidgwick and Jackson Limited
1 Tavistock Chambers, Bloomsbury Way
London WC1A 2SG*

CONTENTS

❁

The dates given in brackets are those of the original publication of the contributions

INTRODUCTION

When the Historical Association invited me to edit a volume of pamphlets on the Tudor period, and to add an article of my own, it was fully recognized that these publications were governed by no central theme. Instead, they represented some of the major – and sometimes controversial – issues of the period which had attracted the research interests of distinguished historians and which successive editors of the Historical Association had felt should be included in the general series. To these we have added Professor Myers's stimulating article on Richard III. The result, as gathered together in this volume, represents some of the important recent trends in Tudor studies.

For many, the most striking feature of the whole period is the interplay between tradition and change. This is reflected not simply in the developments of the sixteenth century itself but in the work of modern historians who have written on the period. The article by Professor A. R. Myers on *Richard III and the historical tradition* forms therefore an appropriate prelude. For it traces in detail the changing conception of Richard III as it emerged among the men of his own time, and as it developed and changed, and changed again, in the succeeding centuries. As we follow the still active controversies about Richard Crookback we see how slender are the surviving facts about crucial events in his life and how tenuous the framework within which historical judgements about him have been erected. No less important, the critical student of the history and the historians of the past becomes increasingly aware that five centuries of writers who have written – and quarrelled – about Richard III, have in the process told us as much about themselves and the assumptions of their society as about Richard III.

If Henry VIII remains at least as controversial as Richard

III, he has succeeded in the present century in attracting outstanding scholars to explore his character and achievements as
a monarch. A. F. Pollard's biography, first published in 1902,
remains after seven decades a masterpiece in its shape and
style. It is examined in detail by Professor Elton below. Here
a brief comment must suffice. Pollard had himself experienced
at first hand the conditions of party politics and had, in
addition, spent many years in the thick of academic politics,
that microcosm of all the idealism, self-sacrifice, hypocrisy,
and pettiness which are to be found in the wider world of state
affairs. He *understood* the nature of the political animal; and,
though modern research has challenged or superseded some of
his generalizations, his book rewards the reader with a subtle
comprehension of Henry's character and policy. Pollard was
too shrewd a man of affairs to fall into the trap of confusing
law with justice. He saw better than did his nineteenth-century
predecessors that the king's almost neurotic obsession with
maintaining the forms of law, or creating new ones when
necessary, was something quite separate from any notion of
justice to dissenting individuals; indeed, the law itself could
be used to deprive the individual of justice and crush diversity
of opinion. Pollard's conclusion was that where the individual
conflicted with the state, Henry was concerned with the preser-
vation of the state at the expense of the individual.

Yet, built into Pollard's scholarly and sceptical study of
Henry VIII there was the basic assumption that the king
served and represented the interests of the people of England
as a whole. No less scholarly, but more sceptical, is Professor
Scarisbrick's view of the king. In his *Henry VIII*, published in
1968, he showed over and over again how the personal interest
of the monarch conflicted with the public interest of the nation;
but at the same time this was a monarch who, with all his
many faults, retained a strong grasp on policy. Professor Lacey
Baldwin Smith, in a novel approach, attempted to reach the
king through the complex processes of psychology. His evidence
in some places proved inadequate and psychological theory was

no substitute for it; but his book, concerned mainly with the last years of Henry's life, was important in showing the strength and authority of the king himself during the period.*

Professor G. R. Elton's work, however, with his unrivalled mastery of the administrative materials of the period, set the pattern of a good deal of recent research on the king and his government. He has never published a full-length biography of Henry VIII; but in one sense he has been writing about him and the Tudor state for many years. His short study of the king, here reprinted, displays with all his vigour and originality his judgement of king and state.

Beneath the question of our assessment of the king there lies the fundamental issue of the nature of Tudor authority, and therefore the central and controversial question of freedom and consent.† These are far too large to be examined in a brief introduction; but in many places in the essays which follow there will be heard echoes of battles won and lost in the Tudor period and in our own debates about that period.

We have so far been considering one of the great themes of the period, the place of the monarch in the early Tudor state; and it has been examined from the centre. Professor Bindoff's essay looks at the position in the middle of the century and from the viewpoint of provincial England. It is here that the complexity as well as the weakness of Tudor authority emerges. For peace and order – the ideal of Tudor governors – depended on a stable distribution of power in the shires and at the centre; and it was precisely this stability during the mid-Tudor period which was far to seek. Professor Bindoff skilfully displays the crumbling of authority in Norfolk coinciding with the decay of authority at the centre during the corrupt and factious reign of Edward VI. The central government under a new minister, the Earl of Warwick, regained the initiative but the built-in weakness of the Tudor crown, its dependence upon a strong

* *The Mask of Royalty*, 1971.
† I discuss some of these questions in my *Freedom, Corruption and Government in Elizabethan England*, to appear in 1973.

personality, becomes clearly visible to the historian, as indeed it did to a good many contemporaries.

The Tudors never wholly cast off the conditions of insecurity which had now become manifest; but this resulted not simply from the faults and cracks in the constitutional structure. It was the result too, as Professor Bindoff shows, of the economic strain and the religious tension which had been building up for decades, indeed longer than that.

The economic crisis of the time and the acute problem of inflation were themselves part of a population crisis whose character is only now being unravelled by historians. The results are mainly being published in contributions to learned journals, beginning with the famous articles by Professor E. H. Phelps-Brown and Miss Sheila Hopkins in *Economica* for 1955 and 1957. Two short modern works, Dr R. B. Outhwaite's *Inflation in Tudor and early Stuart England* (1969) and Professor Peter Ramsey's *The Price Revolution in sixteenth-century England* (1971), lucidly survey and present the results of their own, and other scholars', researches.

To ordinary people, the manifest signs of their economic ills lay in the price rise and secondly in the agrarian crises. Crises in one sense, may be too strong a word to use of the diverse, uneven series of agrarian adjustments which had begun long before the sixteenth century and endured long after it. Dr Joan Thirsk has dealt with many of its features in important scholarly books and articles and in her editorship of a major combined study, *The Agrarian History of England and Wales*, vol. IV, 1500–1640 (1967). As the result of her own work and that of other historians, referred to in her essay *Tudor Enclosures* here published, we can form a better assessment than was once possible of the degree of dislocation and suffering imposed by agrarian change; and we can see also how welcome and rewarding were some of the new approaches to land distribution and use. But she does not minimize the effects upon the people who were hurt most in those midland regions vulnerable to the new pressures.

The great debate about the measurable effects of these changes has lasted a long time and is by no means over; the statistical material, however well exploited and by the most sophisticated means, will probably always prove inadequate for a definitive answer. In any case men riot, not simply because their stomachs are empty but because they are afraid that they will be, under stress of the intrusive forces of economic progress: the fears and assumptions of a community provide an ingredient of a major social problem, but an ingredient elusive to the historian. It would, of course, be a mistake to treat these agrarian changes in purely social and economic terms. R. H. Tawney, in his masterly studies of these problems, drew attention long ago to the need to see them also in respect of legal rights and processes. But he saw them in perspective. For neither the legal nor social explanation alone can reveal the immensely complex issues involved.

Men also riot for non-material reasons of which the most important in the past has always been religion. In *John Knox*, one of the turbulent figures of the Reformation, Professor J. D. Mackie sets forth some of its dominating problems. He sees developments in Scotland as part of a world movement of Reformation, which included faith and confidence, ferocity and intolerance; and all these were marked features of Knox and the Protestant Scotland that he tried to establish. Professor Mackie indeed sees Knox as one of the great formative influences upon the Scottish Reformation and society. In his view, Knox fully expressed and developed those qualities in his fellow countrymen which enabled 'the children of a small, poor country to set their mark on the history of the world'.

Since this brief biography was written we have three valuable standard works on the Reformation: Professor A. G. Dickens's *The English Reformation* (1964), Professor Gordon Donaldson's *The Scottish Reformation* (1960), and Professor Glanmor Williams's *The Welsh Church from Conquest to Reformation* (1962). But what developments were taking place at the border between England and Scotland, the scene of so many bloody battles in the past? We know a good deal more about that Tudor border thanks to the work of various scholars, especially Mr M. E. James's 'Obedience and dissent in Henrician England,' and Dr Claire Cross's *The Puritan Earl* (1966). In Mr F. W. Brooks's article on *The Council of the North* there is clearly brought out the interplay between an evolving, and characteristic, Tudor institution and a changing social order. The Council and the whole Tudor system of government shuddered under the impact of two major upheavals, the Pilgrimage of Grace of 1536 and the Northern Rebellion of 1569. The government survived, partly because its limited resources of men and material could be brought, on these and other critical occasions, to focus on a point of danger. But it survived also through the skilful use of the threat of force (instead of force itself, where possible) and, increasingly, through its mastery of the arts of persuasion. But there remained throughout a community of interest between the Crown and the government class which Elizabeth, more than any of her Tudor predecessors, managed to express and the early Stuarts managed to destroy.

The search for stability amidst diversity and discord provided the main features of the period; and we see them reflected in the work of its greatest poet and playwright. Our final essay is included to give a brief impression of the Tudor world as it was drawing to a close. It may perhaps serve also to remind those who are just embarking on a study of the period that in late Elizabethan and Jacobean literature they have not only a storehouse of never-failing delight but, if they use it with skill and care, a valuable historical source which will enlarge their knowledge even as it extends their vision.

JOEL HURSTFIELD

Certain minor revisions have, where necessary, been made by the authors of each section. They alone are responsible for the views expressed in their contributions and bibliographies.

* *Past and Present* no. 48 (1970), pp. 3–78.

PART ONE

Richard III and Historical Tradition

RICHARD III AND HISTORICAL TRADITION[1]

by

A. R. MYERS

The aim of this article is to investigate the attitudes of
historians to the traditions which grew up about Richard III.
There is abundant material, for there has never been a generation between his day and ours when more than one historian
has not written about him. Now Mr E. H. Carr has told us
that each generation must re-write its history, since the historical perspective can never remain the same. Even if we do not
travel so far along the road of historical relativism as he and
others appear to do, we must nevertheless surely recognize
that the writing of history is itself not immune from change;
as with architecture, what may seem to one generation the
obvious mode of expression may, to a succeeding age, bear the
stamp of a particular time and place. It may therefore be of
interest to examine how far the views on Richard III have
been affected by changes in the climate of opinion between the
sixteenth century and the twentieth.[2] It seems to be a peculiarly
suitable subject for this kind of investigation; for the genius of
Shakespeare has given immortality to a view of Richard III
which was profoundly influenced by the political and emotional
needs of Tudor England. The Shakespearian view has sometimes been accepted in a very sophisticated way, such as that
of Max Buedinger, who held that 'however little the noble
poetry of Shakespeare may agree in detail with the results of
historical research, fundamentally both reach the same goal'.[3]
It has probably been much more common for Shakespeare's
portrait to be accepted as history in a straightforward sense,
whether by men like the great Duke of Marlborough, who is

said to have remarked: 'Shakespeare, the only history I ever read', or even by contemporary historians like Sir Harold Nicolson.[4] Yet this view was largely the result of the conditions of the Tudor state and was therefore likely to be challenged when those conditions had ceased to obtain.

There is no time for a detailed examination of how the Tudor tradition of Richard III developed and fortunately there is no need, for the fame of Shakespeare has led many scholars to address themselves to this problem.[5] All that I need do, before we go forward to the relatively unexplored historiography of later centuries, is to remind you how greatly this tradition, this saga as G. B. Churchill usefully calls it, developed in the hundred years between the death of Richard and the composition of Shakespeare's play about him. The title of Henry VII was so weak and there were so many conspiracies against him that he needed all the justification for his accession that he could find; and the blacker his predecessor's character could be made to appear, the more justified appeared to be his overthrow by Henry. The threats to the Tudor dynasty continued from within and from without England until nearly the end of Elizabeth's reign; and so the need to uphold strenuously the title of Henry VII remained. As Bishop Stubbs rightly observed: 'Richard left none behind him whose duty or whose care it was to attempt his vindication.'[6] It might be necessary to remember the good features of the claim and reign of Edward IV, the father of Henry VII's queen; all could agree in denouncing the villainy of Richard III. As the years went by, the actual events of his reign faded from living memory; and the exact nature of some of the most important had always been obscure. Helped not only by political requirements but by prevalent notions of sudden disaster as an expression of divine judgement on wickedness, the saga rapidly became at once more coherent and more fantastic. Its growth is striking, whether we look at particular episodes or at the picture as a whole.

For particular episodes it may suffice to remind you of the stories about the deaths of Edward of Lancaster at Tewkesbury in 1471 and of George, Duke of Clarence in 1478. Contemporary or near contemporary accounts of the Battle of Tewkesbury describe Prince Edward as having been slain in the field or in flight from it. Perhaps in such a matter we can refuse to accept the silent smoothness of *The Arrival of Edward IV*, an official Yorkist version intended as an apologia to foreign governments; but the same cannot be our reaction to contemporaries such as John Warkworth or the Tewkesbury chronicler, who are rather critical of the Yorkist leaders, or Philippe de Commines, who almost certainly derived his similar information from Lancastrian refugees in Burgundy. But Fabyan's chronicle, finished in 1504, and the *Great Chronicle of London*, completed in 1512, say that Prince Edward was brought before the king after the battle and killed by Edward IV's attendants in cold blood for his bold retort. Then Polydore Vergil added to this by naming Gloucester among the murderers. Edward Hall, whose influential Chronicle was published in 1542, worked this up into a vividly dramatic scene; and so we reach the Shakespearian picture of a captive, but spirited, youth, struck down by Edward IV for his courageous words, and stabbed to death as he lies defenceless on the ground, Gloucester giving the lead in this dastardly act. Or take the death of Clarence in 1478. Contemporaries are silent about any connection of Gloucester with the event, and an Italian visitor to England in 1483, Domenico Mancini, who was hostile to Richard, says flatly that everyone considered the Woodvilles responsible for Clarence's fate. Even after Richard's death, writers who were anxious to blacken his memory still do not associate him with Clarence's execution. Such are John Rous, the Warwick chaplain, who dedicated his *Historia Regum Anglie* to Henry VII, and described Richard as 'a monster and tyrant, born under a hostile star and perishing like Antichrist'; or Bernard André, historiographer royal of Henry VII, whose *Life of Henry VII* depicts him as saintly as Richard was evil. Then Sir Thomas More reported, as a rumour only, the suggestion that Richard was glad of Clarence's death and by secret expressions helped it on; but cautiously added that conjecture may as well shoot too far as too short. Edward Hall copied More's statement but added 'but this conjecture afterwarde took place', by which he apparently means that Richard had desired the crown even while his brother was alive. By the time that *The Mirror for Magistrates* was published in 1559, it had become the accepted view that Richard was Clarence's murderer – murderer not only in the sense of seeing to the execution but murderer in the sense of secretly stirring up Edward's suspicion and wrath against him while publicly pretending to intercede for him. And so again we begin to see the details of Shakespeare's picture.

And what of Shakespeare's portrait of the whole man, deformed from birth both in body and soul, who confides to us in *Henry VI* part III, act 3, scene 2, that he will have the English crown 'Or hew my way out with a bloody axe. Why, I can smile, and murder whiles I smile', and in the first speech of *Richard III* tells us: 'I am determined to prove a villain and hate the idle pleasures of these days. Plots have I laid, inductions dangerous'? Elements of this portrait appeared almost as soon as Richard was dead. Rous's *Historia Regum Anglie*, apparently written between November 1489 and June 1491, speaks of 'the tyrant King Richard, who was born ... after being retained two years in his mother's womb, issuing forth with teeth and hair down to his shoulders', the right shoulder being higher than the left; Rous accuses him of murdering Henry VI, his two nephews, and his wife. But these accusations were not worked into a consistent picture. This was first done in More's history. 'The work not only gives in minute detail an account of all the important events from the death of Edward IV to the outbreak of Buckingham's rebellion, but it presents the most finished portrait of Richard's person and character. Added to this is a style which has caused it to be considered the first piece of historical writing in modern English that has just claim to be called literature.'[7] It is in More that we first get a vivid picture of Richard's diabolical appearance; it is in his history that the King for the first time becomes 'croke backed Richard', the name by which he was known to many generations.

Next to More's biography, the history of Polydore Vergil is of greatest importance in the development of the Richard saga. Vergil provided the account of Richard's early life and the pattern of fifteenth-century history[8]; in this sequence the long tragedy of the Lancastrian versus Yorkist struggle provoked for each crime a divine retribution that could only end if the process culminated in an utter villain, so wicked that his death would be not another crime but a good deed, finally freeing England from its curse. More's portrait and Vergil's pattern were fused together by Edward Hall, who constantly embellishes his originals to bring out the cruelty and wickedness of Richard. To this exaggerated denigration of him was opposed an exaggerated praise of Henry VII, so that, as E. W. M. Tillyard has said: 'for Hall these two are not so much historical personages as Good King and Bad King respectively'.[9] Henry Tudor was now so much the divinely appointed deliverer that the wedding of Henry and Elizabeth of York was gravely compared with the union of godhead and manhood in Jesus Christ; and Buckingham is led to recognize the claim of Henry Tudor to the throne by the working of the Holy Ghost. The *Mirror for Magistrates* added the element that Richard had plotted long before his brother's death to gain the Crown; and so the ground was prepared for the Shakespearian view of Richard as from birth to death the personification of villainy. By the end of the sixteenth century the facts of his real appearance, character, and deeds had been buried under a great mound of tradition. He had become the archetypal tyrant-king, incarnate evil enthroned.

Although this tradition had been the creation of Tudor England, it was not to be expected that it would disappear as soon as the Tudor dynasty had come to an end. Shakespeare himself exercised great influence. In 1614 for example, the poet Christopher Brooke produced a long and gloomy poem called *The Ghost of Richard III,* which only too fully made good its claim to contain 'more of him than hath been heretofore showed either in chronicles, plays, or poems'. It reveals the strong influence of Shakespeare's conception of Richard on the mind of the poet, who frequently uses lines and phrases from the play.* Then there was the fact that the title of James I derived from Margaret Tudor and hence from Henry VII; and a too vigorous rehabilitation of Richard III would have had the dangerous effect of questioning the present king's claim to the throne. There was, of course, a little more room for criticism. In his *History of the World* Sir Walter Raleigh ventured to apply the idea of retribution, so popular in Tudor days, to Henry VII himself; his ingratitude to Sir William Stanley, who was said to have crowned Henry on Bosworth field, was punished in the barrenness of all the king's grandchildren.[10] And Raleigh also denounced the arbitrary acts of Henry VIII. But Raleigh was careful to flatter James I 'who, as well in divine as human understanding, hath exceeded all that forewent him, by many degrees'; and this involved a defence of the title of the Tudors and condemnation of Richard III, 'the greatest master in mischief of all that forewent him', who was cut off by Henry VII, the immediate instrument of God's justice.[11] Bacon and Habington, in spite of their unwillingness to accept all the charges made against Richard III, agreed in believing that the saga, both in general and in detail, was essentially true; and the learned Camden could say of him 'he is by all persons of reflection esteemed a bad man' – though he added 'but a good king'.[12]

One there was who during the reign of James I published a defence of Richard III. This was Sir William Cornwallis who in 1617 printed an essay entitled 'The Praise of King Richard III', but in a volume called *Essays of Certain Paradoxes*. His essay was really a testimony to the continued strength of Tudor tradition; for the titles of Cornwallis's other essays give a taste of his manner, e.g. 'The Praise of the Emperor Julian the Apostate', 'The Praise of the French Pockes', etc. His essay in

---

* It contained, in fact, a tribute to Shakespeare in the second section (p. 27).

defence of Richard III was not meant to be taken seriously; it was an exercise in rhetoric to defend the indefensible.

Another apologia for Richard III was written between 1605 and 1621 by Sir George Buc, an Elizabethan and Jacobean courtier of varied accomplishments; but it was not printed until 1646, when his nephew published it in his own name. It is more important than Cornwallis's essay, for it was meant to be taken seriously and is much more detailed. It is as comprehensive a defence as the saga is an attack. Buc clears the King of every charge made against him; he denies that Richard was a villain and asserts that on the contrary he was a good king whose memory had been blackened by Tudor historians. Buc was an antiquary of some note, a member of the first Society of Antiquaries;* and it may be through the contacts of this society, especially Sir Robert Cotton, that he was able to consult many of the Cotton MSS. and the public records. He produced weighty evidence from the Croyland Continuator and the Titulus Regius in the Rolls of Parliament that Edward IV's alleged pre-contract of marriage had been with Eleanor Butler and not with Elizabeth Lucy, as More had said. He refers to other documents which at first sight seem striking evidence against the tradition of Richard's utter villainy. For example, so far from Princess Elizabeth being constrained to marry her uncle, she had written a letter in which she looked forward with pleasure to such a marriage; Buc alleges that he had seen this letter in the Earl of Arundel's collection of MSS. But it is hard to accept Buc's testimony on this, for no one else has ever seen this document, or others that he quotes; and where his use of documents can be checked, he is found to have been sometimes careless in the handling of their testimony. In fact, except for

* The Society's interest in English medieval history is generally thought to have been the chief reason for its sudden disappearance; for James I is said to have mistrusted its investigations into the origins of Parliament (Joan Evans, *A History of the Society of Antiquaries*, 1956, p. 13). See also the unpublished thesis of Dr Linda van Norden, 'The Elizabethan College of Antiquaries' (University of California, Los Angeles, 1946).

his criticism of More, Buc's defence of Richard III does not amount to much.

It is, however, of more interest for the light it throws on the methods of English historical scholarship in his day. It was an age of great erudition but little critical method; even so learned a scholar as John Milton could write the early history of Britain entirely in terms of Geoffrey of Monmouth's legends of Brut and Lear and Lud and the rest, because he found that tradition so well established. Buc's work is immensely erudite and extremely diffuse. Every fancied parallel and example from history is brought in, with often far-fetched citations at every turn, from classical authors to writers of his own day. At the least excuse he wanders into long digressions, with erudite but usually misguided etymologies. Thus the mention of Richard Plantagenet, father of Richard III, triggers him off to make a long digression into the origin of the name. He says that the Plantagenet badge was first adopted by Fulk of Anjou when he went on pilgrimage to the Holy Land in A.D. 1000 to expiate his crimes. Buc remarks how suitable it was that Fulk should take the broom plant for his badge, since Pliny tells us that the genista was medicinal for complaints of the genu, the knee, on which one kneels, and so it is a sign of humility; and 'as Strabo relates', the genista grows in the sandy wastes of the Holy Land and was therefore very apt for Fulk's scouring as a penitent at the Holy Sepulchre.[13] Then in Book 4 of his work Buc asks why Edward IV did not take the precaution of having the legitimacy of his children safeguarded by Act of Parliament; at once the author slips into an excursion on the origins of Parliament and the meaning of the word. On this he quotes one authority (this time unnamed), who had said that 'the word Parliament is compounded of *Parium* and *lamentum*, because, as he thinketh, the Peers of the Country did at these Meetings complain each to other of the Enormities of their Country'.[14] These examples not only show that Buc could not keep to the point. They demonstrate that he, along with the other scholars of his time, had no adequate methods of historical criticism. His favourite way of dealing with legends about Richard is not to examine their credentials but to counter them with some other reputed instance or document. Thus in answer to Rous's story that Richard was born with teeth, he quotes Plutarch, Livy, Valerius Maximus, and Pliny for stories of good men who were born with semi-circular bones in their mouths instead of teeth; and in reply to the story of Richard's share in the murder of Edward of Lancaster he says: 'but to the contrary I have seen in a faithful Manuscript Chronicle of those times, that the Duke of Gloucester only of all the great Persons stood still and drew not his Sword'.[15] No one else has ever seen this document; but Buc was not peculiar in his inability to weigh historical evidence. The Titulus Regius in the Rolls of Parliament on which Buc set so much store in refuting More was quoted by Speed, Prynne, and Camden. In none of these distinguished scholars did it arouse any queries as to the credibility of More, or the Tudor tradition. John Strype, who supplied notes to Buc's biography, was content to reject his author's documented arguments by recalling the versions of More, Hall, and Holinshed. Any document could be countered by almost any other document, provided that the latter was old, and hallowed by tradition.

It is well known that documents illustrative of parliamentary or church history could be used in seventeenth-century controversy without much sense of the passage of time and the change of circumstances; this happened to the documents of the Richard saga and to the saga itself. Thus Prynne reprinted the Titulus Regius in 1656 to oppose Cromwell, who was supposed to be aiming at the Crown, by showing how a tyrant had sought 'to gain and settle the Kingship on him by such Politick Stratagems'.[16] The saga was more often used to back royalist propaganda. Thus in 1649 'T. W., Gentleman' published *Plantagenet's Tragicall Story or the Death of Edward IV with the unnaturall voyage of Richard III through the Red Sea of his Nephews' innocent blood to his usurped Crowne*. The tract aims to show how damnable was the man who ought to have been the pillar of the throne and yet conspired to overthrow the lawful king. The truth of the saga is assumed and Tyrrell as the chief murderer is specially execrated as he prepares to murder the princes:

> A wreath of Snakes (instead of hair) did crawl
> About his head, and down his shoulders fall;
> A basilisk did look through either eye.
> His face annealed by the flames that flye
> From Hell's sulphurous tomb; about his neck
> A chain of Curses hang, and at his back
> Waiteth Repentance (ready to depart)
> With tear-swoln eyes, and Vultures at her heart;
> In his hands he holdeth a Commission
> Written in blood by th' Prince of Acheron.[17]

The Richard saga could be evoked on behalf of royalism in happier circumstances. In 1666 a play that has survived in many copies was put on at the Duke of York's Theatre in London, entitled *The English Princess or the Death of Richard III*. Richard III is repeatedly referred to as 'the Tyrant' and is clearly compared to Cromwell. The English Princess is Elizabeth of York who, it is emphasized, has the legitimist claim to the Crown and is rescued partly by loyal borderers – shades, no doubt, of General Monck. The moral is pushed home by the Epilogue which says:

> Richard is dead and now begins your Reign;
> Let not the Tyrant live in you again.
> For though one Tyrant be a Nation's Curse,
> Yet Commonwealths of Tyrants are much worse;
> Their Name is Legion: And a Rump (you know)
> In Cruelty all Richards doth outgo.*

* To enhance the dignity of legitimist monarchy, it is Princess Elizabeth who in scene 10 orders Sir William Stanley to place the crown on Richmond's head, as a conqueror, after Henry has asked her to wear it by hereditary right.

Richard III's usurpation was also cited repeatedly in the excitements of the Exclusion agitations of 1679–81. Though some of the anti-Exclusionist writers emphasized the hereditary right of Richard III and the supposedly bad effects of the parliamentary title of Henry VII,[18] in the main the saga was still accepted without question. Buc's defence had made no impression. It might be discounted as the result of family pride; for, as he is careful to tell us in another long digression, his ancestor had fought for Richard at Bosworth. In any event the discovery in 1674 in the Tower of London of the bones which were assumed to be those of the princes and were buried as such in Westminster Abbey seemed to contemporaries to be a striking corroboration of More's story.

It is well known how much English historical scholarship in the seventeenth century was influenced by the desire to settle controversies. Some of it was of a high order like Selden's *Mare Clausum*, to prove England's claim to the sovereignty of the seas, or Spelman's *History and Fate of Sacrilege*, to support a legal and moral argument against the dissolution of the monasteries. Some of it was the fruit of long and sustained labours like the parliamentary antiquities of William Prynne or the *Anglia Sacra* of Henry Wharton. All showed much erudition. But English historical scholarship lacked the critical spirit which, after the days of Ducange and Mabillon, began to pervade that of France. At the end of the century England could produce Madox; but even so devoted a scholar as Rymer could print a spurious homage of Malcolm II to Edward the Confessor. The new spirit took even longer to affect the general histories of England; the first in which it is clearly to be seen is, not surprisingly, the work of a Huguenot refugee.

This was Paul Rapin de Thoyras,[19] who in 1723 and 1725 published the two volumes of a history of England that remained a standard account for a quarter of a century. A French lawyer who honourably refused forcible conversion to Catholicism in 1685, he took refuge in England in 1686, afterwards enlisted in Holland, returned to England with the troops of William of Orange, and became tutor in 1693 to the Duke of Portland's eldest son. Then some years later he went back to the Netherlands, where he came very much under the influence of that pioneer historian of the Age of Reason, Pierre Bayle. In some ways Rapin was irrational, as indeed were his successors in the Age of Reason. He held, for example, that English government had not changed fundamentally since the days of the Saxons, and he seems to have been one of the authors from whom Montesquieu derived the idea that English liberty had been founded in the forests of Germany. But he shows himself critical of some historical traditions that had been generally accepted until then. After reviewing in a mere twenty-four lines the beginnings of British history according to Geoffrey of Monmouth (which John Milton had retailed in over eighty folio pages), Rapin concludes: 'But it brings with it so many Marks of Forgery, that it is looked upon by all that have examined it with any attention, as a Fiction of Geoffrey himself or of some Author whom he has too implicitly followed.'[20] And so after recounting the traditional tale of the murder of Edward of Lancaster by Richard and other Yorkists after Tewkesbury, he comments: 'But I do not know whether the Historians are to be credited who affirm that these four Lords killed the Prince with their own hands. This might be an effect of the prejudice of those that wrote the history after the res-toration of the house of Lancaster since it is certain they have forgotten nothing to render the house of York odious.' This is the kind of scepticism one does not find in Buc's defence of Richard III. Of course, one must not expect the new critical spirit to triumph completely in a single work. Most of Rapin's picture of Richard III was, in fact, a cautious acceptance of the traditional story; and he can even say that 'Richard III was sirnamed Crook-back'd because he was so in reality.'[21] He thought that Richard was a good man corrupted by ambition, a danger to which he considered rulers to be especially liable.

Once the question of the saga had begun, however, it was taken up by various historians on other points. In 1736 Francis

Drake, Yorkshire antiquarian, published his *Eboracum: or the History and Antiquities of the City of York*, supported by hitherto unprinted records. The evidence that he found forced him to conclude that Richard had been liked and respected in the north and that his bad reputation must have been due to Tudor propaganda. Then the Whig historian and pamphleteer, William Guthrie, published a *General History of England* between 1744 and 1751.* He stresses repeatedly that one must be very cautious before opposing the consensus of historical opinion on a period or problem; but he is even more doubtful than Rapin about the truth of the saga. He thought that Richard probably did not murder Henry VI and advanced various queries as to the truth of More's story of the murder of the Princes in the Tower. Shortly after Guthrie's history was published, there appeared the more scholarly work of Thomas Carte,[22] a Jacobite non-juring clergyman who, like Hearne, had to work hard at his historical writing to make a living. Rapin and Guthrie had, in the main, still held that the traditional view of Richard III was essentially true; but Carte, although conceding that Richard's seizure of the throne and the executions that accompanied it were great crimes, was emphatic that the King was innocent of all the other evil deeds of which he was accused, including the murder of his nephews. By the middle of the century only one major author stood out against the general trend towards increasing scepticism about the saga. This was David Hume, whose *History of England* remained influential until well into the nineteenth century.† Hume may be justly famous as a philosopher; but as a historian he does not deserve to be taken so seriously as his contem-

* His chief activity was that of a Whig pamphleteer. He thought that Edward IV was more culpable than Richard III, because Edward had corrupted public life by his sexual immorality and his arbitrary taxation.
† From conversations with Sir Winston Churchill, when he was writing *A History of the English-Speaking Peoples*, vol. I, I learnt that Hume's History was still being read for instruction at Harrow in the 1880s. Cf. W. S. Churchill, *My Early Life* (1930), p. 124: 'I had always liked history at school. But there we were given only the dullest, driest pemmicanized forms like *The Student's Hume*.'

poraries, especially on this matter. For one thing he did not regard this period as worthy of serious investigation. It is significant that he left until the last the writing of the history of medieval England, which was published in 1761; his work on the period 1603 to 1688 had been printed in 1754 and that on the Tudors had appeared in 1759. His account of medieval England ended with the story of Bosworth Field and the characteristic comment: 'Thus have we pursued the history of England through many barbarous ages; till we have at last reached the dawn of civility and science and have the prospect both of greater certainty in our narrations and of being able to present to the reader a spectacle more worthy of his attentions.'[23] He was willing to spend neither time nor research on the medieval part of his history; it was written in a few months and a Scottish friend said of him: 'Why, mon, David read a vast deal before he set about a piece of his book; but his usual seat was the sofa, and he often wrote with his legs up; and it would have been unco' fashious to have moved across the room when any little doubt occurred.'[24] He found the saga presented in nearly all the histories and it was easier to accept it than to question it. Its view of Richard III as a born villain was acceptable, since nothing was too bad to have happened in the monkish, barbarous Middle Ages.[25]

David Hume might differ from many of his contemporaries about the character of Richard III; but he shared with them the preconceptions of the age about the past. There was a prevalent idea that men are dominated by 'ruling passions' which produce a fundamental consistency in a person's nature.* It was commonly assumed that all men, in all periods and in all

* D. A. Stauffer, *The Art of Biography in Eighteenth Century England*, 1941, pp. 323–7, 338–40, 539. Cf. A. Pope, *An Epistle to Richard, Lord Cobham*, 1733, pp. 9–10.
> 'Find, if you can, in what you cannot change.
> 'Tis in the *ruling passion*; there, alone,
> The wild are constant and the cunning known.
> The fool consistent, and the false sincere
> Priests, princes, women, no dissemblers here.'

Also his *Essay on Man*, Epistle 2, section 3, lines 130–74.

countries were fundamentally the same, and that in the past the standards and springs of behaviour had been at bottom those of the mid-eighteenth century, though they had been grossly misrepresented by historians of former ages. It was also thought that unless their judgement was distorted by prejudice, superstition and ignorance, men of quality in any period could be presumed to act according to the dictates of enlightened and rational self-interest.* In the historiography of Richard III during this period these traits are very apparent. Guthrie and Carte both agree that the saga cannot be true because Richard is there described as performing acts to his own hurt, which is out of character with his conduct at other times and his nature as a shrewd and cunning man. They relied on pieces of forensic rhetoric, such as, for example, the argument that only a fool, in Richard's shoes, would have murdered the Princes in the Tower, and Richard was not a fool.

All these authors had written of Richard III as part of a work whose theme transcended this – whether a history of England or a history of York. Horatio, or Horace, Walpole, however, in his *Historic Doubts on the Life and Reign of King Richard III* (1767) was dealing solely with Richard III. Walpole is especially fascinating in the contrasts and complexities of his personality. In one aspect of his character he was very much a man of his time – elegant, critical, very closely involved in the governing society of his age, a man of taste anxious not to display any ill-bred enthusiasm. Underneath this exterior, he was warm-hearted and hated injustice.[26] He was aware of the comparison drawn in the 1750s between Richard III and William, Duke of Cumberland, who was thought to be aspiring to the throne at the expense of his nephew, later George III; and in a letter to Henry Fox, Walpole referred to

* See, for example, D. Hume, *Enquiry concerning the Human Understanding* (1777), section 8, part I (e.g. 'Mankind are so much the same, in all times and places that history informs us of nothing new or strange in this particular. Its chief use is only to discover the constant and universal principles of human nature.'), and *History of England*, vol. 3, 1780, pp. 301–9.

doggerel verses on the subject that were being privately circulated.[27] But this topical interest in Richard III was reinforced by
more unusual motives. Ahead of his times, Walpole could be
attracted to the Middle Ages, fill the gothicized Strawberry
Hill with copies of medieval work, and admire the rediscovered
Paston Letters. His hatred of injustice, coupled with his interest
in the Middle Ages, eventually led him to write a book to
show how weak was the case for the Tudor saga. He was, however, sufficiently a man of his time to want to avoid any suspicion of 'enthusiasm', and said that he was merely airing his
doubts; but the effect was of a whole-hearted defence of
Richard III as thorough as that of Buc. Walpole was, however,
much too well known to be saved from comment by his de-
precating attitude; and the book aroused a storm of criticism
from various quarters, including Guthrie, Hume, Gibbon, and
a lawyer, Guydickens.[28] The criticisms that Walpole resented
most were those of a Fellow of the Society of Antiquaries,
Robert Masters, who attacked his arguments in detail, and of
the President of the Society, Dr Jeremiah Milles, Dean of
Exeter.[29] In dealing with the murder of the Princes, Walpole
had triumphantly cited a document which, he claimed, was the
Coronation Roll of Richard III and proved that Edward V
was then not only alive but sufficiently free and honoured
to walk in Richard's coronation procession. Dr Milles wrote
a review in which he showed that the prized 'Coronation Roll'
was nothing of the kind, but a wardrobe account, which merely
demonstrated that preparations had been made for the coronation of Edward V and that the robes made for the young king
had thriftily been used for Richard's son Edward instead. Walpole was very hurt, for he considered it very ill-bred for a
member of a society to attack in public the work of a gentleman
who was a fellow member. He made fun of the pedantry of a
man of learning in the eyes of a man of taste, since Dr Milles
had rather ponderously explained that the document in question
was a book and not a roll. Shortly afterwards the Society heard
a paper on Dick Whittington and his cat, and a few months

later was burlesqued in consequence on the stage of the Haymarket Theatre. Walpole seized the opportunity to resign from the Society, on the grounds that it had made itself ridiculous.*

His brush with Dr Milles, however, had demonstrated the weakness of his book, and indeed of the approach of most historians of that generation to the subject. Walpole had done no work on the sources and so he was forced to try to break down the tradition by rationalist forensic methods. He depended essentially on showing that it would not have been reasonable or in harmony with Richard's usual character for him to have behaved as he was supposed to have done in the saga. A sudden change from worthy public servant to plotting scoundrel was not in accordance with reason. Thus with regard to the disappearance of the Princes in the Tower, Walpole pointed out that Richard was well liked in the north and treated Clarence's children kindly, which was more than Henry Tudor did. Except for Dr Milles, none of Walpole's critics examined sources but opposed him with the same rationalist and forensic type of argument that he himself used. Guthrie, for example, complained that Walpole had carried arguments further than was reasonable; and this mode of thought continued to be dominant in works on the subject – by Hutton, Lemon, Henry, and Laing.[30] Indeed, Malcolm Laing, a distinguished Scottish lawyer, who in 1793 published the sixth volume of Robert Henry's *History of Great Britain* and vigorously defended King Richard by mainly forensic arguments, roundly declared: 'I am unwilling unnecessarily to incriminate human nature.'[31]

It was one of the last utterances of the Age of Reason; for in that very year the optimism of the eighteenth century about human nature was being violently destroyed. In February 1793 Horatio Walpole, now the Earl of Orford, added a *Postscript to*

* See, J. Evans, *op. cit.*, pp. 167–9. In fairness to the Society it ought to be mentioned that the author of the paper on Whittington, Samuel Pegge, was a noted antiquary who made the ingenious suggestion that the cat may have been a ship of the build known by that name.

the Historic Doubts.[32] It was penned in the horror aroused by the Reign of Terror in France and the execution of Louis XVI in December 1792. 'It is', Walpole wrote sadly, 'afflictive to have lived to find in an age called not only civilized but enlightened, in this eighteenth century ... such unparalleled crimes displayed ... in Paris, the rival of Athens and Rome ... that I must now believe that any atrocity may have been attempted or practised by an ambitious prince of the blood aiming at the Crown in the fifteenth century. I can believe (I do not say I do) that Richard Duke of Gloucester dipped his hand in the blood of the saint-like Henry the Sixth, though so revolting and injudicious an act as to excite the indignation of mankind against him. I can now believe that he contrived the death of his own brother Clarence – and I can think it possible, inconceivable as it was, that he aspersed the chastity of his own mother, in order to bastardize the offspring of his eldest brother; for all these extravagant excesses have been exhibited in the compass of five years by a monster, by a royal duke, who has actually surpassed all the guilt imputed to Richard the Third, and who, devoid of Richard's courage, has acted his enormities openly, and will leave it impossible to any future writer, however disposed to candour, to entertain one historic doubt on the abominable actions of Philip, Duke of Orleans.' This postscript is more than the despairing cry of a disillusioned old man; it is in this field the death-rattle of the Age of Reason.

> There are more things in Heaven and earth, Horatio,
> Than are dreamt of in your philosophy.

The Age of Reason, which had on the whole regarded the Middle Ages with contempt, was followed by the Age of Romanticism, which viewed the Middle Ages with admiration; and the memory of Richard III benefited accordingly. As usually happens, the ages overlapped. A few months before Walpole wrote his sorrowful postscript, a young lawyer, Sharon

Turner, then aged twenty-four, who was to become one of
the most distinguished British historians of the Romantic
Revival, spent his summer holidays visiting ancient and medieval sites in Wiltshire, Hampshire, and Dorset. On his road
to Weymouth, where George III was then staying, he spent
the night at the village inn at Cerne Abbas; and there he mused
on the contrast between the peaceful existence of George III,
then taking the waters at Weymouth, and the violent career
of Richard III, as depicted in the saga.[33] Turner resolved to
investigate the Tudor tradition, not only to see that justice
was done, 'but for the right understanding of this portion of
our history'.[34] For the serious interest that he and the rising
generation now took in the Middle Ages made it seem worthy
of industrious investigation and adequate documentation.
Symptomatic of the change which had come over historiography
was the contrast between Hume's neglect of any personal
research on the Middle Ages before he began to write about
them, and the sixteen years of study which Sharon Turner devoted to the preparation of his *History of the Anglo-Saxons*
before he published a word.* He gradually extended his history
to the end of the sixteenth century, but it took him another
twenty-four years to do so. The result was a great advance in
the understanding of these earlier centuries of the country's
history; for Turner not only sought hard for original evidence
but, like many of his generation, he was much more willing
than the men of the Age of Reason to recognize the contrasts
in ways of life and outlook between other ages, other lands, and
his own.

This new outlook had an important effect on the view of
Richard III. Unlike Walpole and his contemporaries, Turner
did not regard the King as a kind of barbarous eighteenth-
century politician, but a man of his time and period. This
brought in many ways a greater realism into the historiography

* His *History of England from the earliest period to the Norman
Conquest* was published in 4 vols. between 1799 and 1805. He had learnt
Anglo-Saxon and Icelandic when he was a boy in order to be able to
study the sources of the period.

. .

of Richard III, as, for instance, the recognition that it was not his unpopularity but 'a perfidious combination of five noblemen which destroyed Richard'.[35] The greater awareness of the conditions of the age tended to lead to a more favourable view of the King. Turner gave a prominent place in his *History* to Richard III, whom he cleared of every accusation against him except the murder of his nephews and the executions related to his accession; and even in these cases it was, he held, violence forestalling violence. Gloucester seized the government because the ambitions of the Woodvilles threatened to keep him from power and perhaps to take away his life and plunge the country into civil war. He deposed Edward V because he feared that the boy was irreconcilably attached by his upbringing to the hostile Woodville group. But this greater understanding of the conditions of the age did not lead to the attitude 'to understand all is to forgive all'. On the contrary, Turner, like so many of his contemporaries, had been deeply influenced by the Evangelical Revival and was a devout Christian who stressed the absolute sanctity of moral principles.* Though he explains Richard's usurpation, he does not condone it. On the contrary, after stating that 'Richard proceeded to the usurpation of the crown, with the approbation of most of the great men, both of the church and state, then in London' he adds: 'Not that the assent of the whole country could be any justification of the treasonable and immoral action; but the preceding facts prove, that the protector, however bad or blameable, was no worse than the most distinguished men of rank of the day.'[36] And Turner's comment on Richard's situation at the beginning of 1485 is: 'Richard began the fatal year of 1485 with a diminution of his own safety, by the very measures which human calculation had

---

* He was, for example, so shocked by what he regarded as Milman's lax views on miracles that in 1832 he published a *Sacred History of the World* in three volumes to defend orthodoxy; and in the preface to his poem on *Richard the Third* he wrote: 'Everyone is morally bound to do at all times what is right, whatever be the tempting or surrounding exigencies.'

2—TT * *

supposed would most firmly consolidate it. Such will be the issue of all policy that is not founded on moral rectitude.'[37] Sometimes the greater interest in and sympathy for this period caused historians to examine whether their moral strictures were justified. Thus Sir Harris Nicolas, while praising in general the work of his great friend Sharon Turner, pointed out that he was wrong to condemn Richard for wearing magnificent clothes. This, he agreed, could rightly have been condemned as betraying a want of seriousness in early Victorian England; but it was a necessity of fifteenth-century kingship. Nicolas, like Turner, showed his respect for the importance of medieval history by paying great attention to the sources; and such attention produced some new facts. Nicolas demonstrated, for example, how untenable were the arguments for the genuineness of Warbeck's claims to be the younger son of Edward IV, as Walpole had pressed. These arguments depended especially on the supposition that Margaret of Burgundy had not been in England since her marriage in 1468 and so could not have coached Warbeck on what Richard Duke of York was like as a child; but Margaret had in fact visited England in 1480, as a wardrobe account clearly proved.[38] And the wealth of references to both literary and official sources in Sharon Turner's work, together with his general shrewdness in the historical criticism of them, is in marked contrast to the much slighter knowledge and interest commonly shown by eighteenth-century writers.

I have devoted a fair amount of time to Sharon Turner because of his importance for this subject. His *History* shows how a sensitive and careful scholar could reflect the influences of his time, and the merits of his work caused it to wield great influence for the next two generations. Early and mid-Victorian England saw the maintenance of considerable interest in and sympathy for Richard III. Several biographies of him were written, of which the most important were those of Miss C. A. Halsted and J. H. Jesse.[39] They also are marked by their wealth of documentation – Miss Halsted has eighty-two appendices covering 128 pages in her two volumes. They both lay stress on the importance of moral principles while emphasizing that Richard must be viewed in relation to his time – which, they pointed out, was not so strict in moral principles as Victorian England. They are not always quite so perceptive of fifteenth-century realities as Sharon Turner and Harris Nicolas; for example, Miss Halsted thought that Richard must have been a remarkable child because he was made Knight of the Garter at the age of nine, and that his seizure of Edward V's attendants at Stony Stratford was quite legal because he had consulted his counsellors before doing it.[40] But both followed Turner and Nicolas in rejecting the saga. They went further and exonerated Richard of all the crimes with which he had been charged and thought that he was a good man corrupted by ambition who had nevertheless saved England from civil war.

This more favourable attitude was widespread in this period, whether in general histories or in specialist works like those of R. Davies, *Extracts from the Municipal Records of the City of York* (1843) and R. Surtees, *History and Antiquity of the County Palatine of Durham* (1812–40), both of which provided evidence of Richard's deserved popularity in the north.[41] The interest in Richard spread to the Continent and both French and German studies of him were published – Jean Rey, *Essais historiques et critiques sur Richard III roi d'Angleterre* (1818) and Max Buedinger, *König Richard III von England* (1858). Both are favourable to Richard; and indeed much of Buedinger's essay was devoted to showing how wide is the contrast between the Richard of Shakespeare and the Richard of history. In fact the only considerable historian of this period who clung to the Tudor historical tradition was John Lingard. As a Roman Catholic priest he had a natural respect for tradition and was impressed in particular by the authority and reputation for truth of Sir Thomas More. Moreover, he wanted to show an apprehensively Protestant England that history written by a Roman Catholic need not be either provocative or revolutionary.* But Lingard was exceptional; it was the general view that the King had been grossly libelled by Tudor historians.

The interest in the past aroused by the Romantic Revival led, as historians know, to a more systematic custody of the records of the past, especially in the Public Record Office, and a more systematic study of English and European history, in the universities and elsewhere. So there developed a wider and more intense respect for professional historical scholarship. This led in the late nineteenth century to a reaction amongst scholars to a more unfavourable view of Richard III. For one of the respected authorities on this period was James Gairdner (1828–1912), a scholar who spent all his working life in the Public Record Office and was deeply versed in the documents of the period, many of which he edited. And in 1878 he published a biography of Richard which once more took the Tudor tradition as its guide. This attitude went back to 1862. In volume I of *Letters and Papers illustrative of the Reigns of Richard III and Henry VII*, published in 1861, Gairdner is quite favourable to Richard; whereas in volume 2, published in 1863, he is already a defender of the traditional view, and makes a scornful reference to the defenders of the King.[42] This change of attitude had come with a deeply felt conversion to Anglo-Catholicism which caused him thenceforth to have, like John Lingard, a great respect for tradition. This is made quite explicit in the preface to his biography of Richard III. He there admits that he, too, had in youth been favourably disposed towards that King, but continues: 'I feel quite ashamed at this day to think how I mused over this subject long ago, wasting a great deal of time, ink, and paper, in fruitless efforts to satisfy even my own mind that traditional black was real

* His main work was his *History of England*, published in eight volumes between 1819 and 1831; and he wrote of it to a friend: 'Through the work I made it a rule to tell the truth, whether it made for us or against us; to avoid all appearance of controversy, that I might not repel protestant readers' (M. Haile and E. Bonney, *Life and Letters of John Lingard*, 1911, p. 166).

historical white, or at worst a kind of grey. At last I laid aside
my incomplete MS. and applied myself to other subjects, still
of a kindred nature; and a larger study of history in other
periods convinced me that my method of starting had been
altogether wrong. The attempt to discard tradition in the
examination of original sources of history is, in fact, like the
attempt to learn an unknown language without a teacher. We
lose the benefit of a living interpreter.'[43] The first conspicuous
application of this conviction in the biography is in his discussion of the death of Edward of Lancaster at Tewkesbury.
After admitting the weakness of the evidence, he nevertheless
states his belief in Gloucester's guilt because of the tradition,
and comments: 'If the murder of Prince Edward was in any
degree attributable to Richard it was doubtless the first of a
long series of crimes, each of which rests on slender testimony
enough, though any one of them, being admitted, lends greater
credit to the others.'[44] This is shaky reasoning indeed, as frail as
is his reliance on tradition in this case. For though historians do
at times have to make use of tradition – sometimes to a considerable extent, as in the history of early Anglo-Saxon England
or modern Africa – it always has to be handled with caution. In
this case its acceptance as the guide to study begs the very question that is to be investigated; for the peculiar problem of
Richard III is how much importance to attach to Tudor
tradition. Yet Gairdner's great reputation for scholarship and
careful editing, and the general respect for specialist historians
of proved competence sufficed to secure the acceptance of his
view by the leading historians of his day, such as J. H. Ramsay,
J. R. Green, C. W. C. Oman, and, in a more cautious form,
Bishop Stubbs. This attitude was reflected in popular historians
like A. O. Legge, who carried on the mid-Victorian tradition
of vigorous moral judgements, but in an unfavourable sense.[45]

There was one influential writer of late Victorian England
who refused to follow Gairdner's lead. Sir Clements Markham
(1830–1916), a man of action, presents the utmost contrast to
Gairdner not only in his views on Richard III but in his

whole career. The son of a parson of good family, he served in the navy and the civil service; and while thus engaged, he visited many parts of the world, including the Pacific Islands and the Arctic, South America and Ethiopia. He explored the Inca ruins of Peru, and performed the feat of transplanting cinchona plants from the slopes of the Andes to the mountains of India, Ceylon and Burma, to improve the world's supplies of quinine. In his later years he was recognized as one of the leading geographers of his time; he was president of the Hakluyt Society for twenty years and president of the Royal Geographical Society for twelve. As well as living a life of action* and dealing with heavy administrative responsibilities, he managed to edit, translate or write some eighty books, dictionaries and papers, including three historical romances and eighteen biographies.[46]

Amongst the latter was his *Life of Richard III*, of which his biographer writes: 'The compilation of this book caused him, probably, greater labour and research than any other work he had written.'[47] Early in his life he had become convinced that the Tudor traditions of Richard III were 'absolute inventions, circulated by the followers and upholders of Henry VII solely for political purposes'. Gairdner's biography stimulated Markham to write a reply; and the result is the most thorough and fervent vindication of Richard that had ever appeared. Even charges that had previously been supposed to be beyond question were vigorously swept aside. Was Hastings executed without trial? Not at all; there was a week's delay after his arrest, which allowed time for a trial.[48] With so just a king, if there was time, it was quite safe to assume that there must have been a fair trial, as there must also for Rivers and Vaughan at Pontefract. And so far from Richard having murdered his nephews, that was undoubtedly the work of the odious villain of the piece – Henry VII. The usual methods of treatment

---

* For example, at the age of seventy-one he had by his influence and energy raised over £93,000 by subscriptions to finance Scott's first Antarctic Expedition (A. H. Markham, *op. cit.*, p. 328).

may be divided into two kinds – demonstrations that Richard was too good a man to commit crimes (which is more than can be said of Henry VII) and repeated stress on the fact that not merely is the evidence against Richard feeble, but the result of a deliberate Tudor plot to blacken his memory. With the most astonishing ingenuity and forensic skill, Markham shows that almost every source has either been suppressed or twisted to serve the conspiracy against Richard – mostly by Cardinal Morton, who seems to have been as ubiquitous as Ariel and as wicked as Caliban. The very thoroughness of Markham works against the credibility of his portrait; it is as impossible to be-lieve in his crowned angel as in Shakepeare's crowned fiend. Markham was a man of action who, to judge from the story of his life and from his numerous biographies, saw men in terms of black and white. Added to this was an early Victorian belief in moral certitudes in the writing of history and the fact that in Markham's impressionable youth the favourable view of Richard was in fashion. The result is that Richard is described as 'the young hero'.[49] Similar expressions are to be found in other biographies of his, such as those of the parliamentary general Fairfax and King Edward VI. There, too, Markham knew no bounds to the defence of his heroes, and part of that defence consisted in denigrating the characters of their rivals. There, too, the most ingenious mental agility is displayed to defend them in every respect; thus though Edward VI could have no hereditary claim to the throne through Henry VIII, since neither Henry VII nor Elizabeth of York had any title to the throne, Edward VI had a good parliament-ary title (though Henry VII had not) and anyway Edward's mother, Jane Seymour, was descended from Edward III.[50] Markham's romantic enthusiasm and Victorian moral fervour make his book fascinating, even compelling, reading. He is still the most persuasive out-and-out defender of Richard III who has yet appeared.

I have devoted so much time to him and to Gairdner be-cause with their rival biographies appears the cleavage that is so often apparent in the twentieth century between the popular views. From Markham are derived the fervour and the arguments of writers like Mr Philip Lindsay* and Miss Josephine Tey, who wrote the best-selling novel about Richard III, *Daughter of Time*. From Markham, too, has been derived the inspiration for that remarkable phenomenon of our time – the societies for the defence of Richard III. In spite of the growing Americanization of British life, it is perhaps significant of remaining differences that the British society in his defence evoked heraldic overtones and was called the Fellowship of the White Boar; whereas the American counterpart combined fraternity and business – 'Friends of Richard III Incorporated'. Is it not remarkable, in view of the counter-attractions of world history, that the rehabilitation of a long-dead king should seem sufficiently important as to attract sustained popular support on both sides of the Atlantic and induce film stars like Miss Helen Hayes and Miss Tallulah Bankhead to become founder members of 'Friends of Richard III Incorporated'? May it not be due in part to the special awareness in our time of the role of government propaganda in the formation of public opinion? To those who have lived through an epoch of Nazi and Communist double-talk and brainwashing, it seems natural for the untrained mind to think of a Tudor government in terms of equal propagandist efficiency. And in an age which has been taught by the popular press that it is both courageous and desirable to be constantly ferreting out the scandals of 'the establishment', is there not a peculiar satisfaction for some in exposing not only the plots of Tudor governments but the obtuseness and the supposed conspiracies of silence of twentieth-century dons? So we have a popular view which, like that of Markham, will have no truck

* 'My most enormous debt is to Sir Clements Markham's *Richard III* ... Here the truth about Richard is plainly given, and all readers who would like a longer and more profound discussion of the subject should read this book' (Philip Lindsay, *King Richard III*, 1934, p. 343). Cf. his *On some Bones in Westminster Abbey: A defence of King Richard III*, 1934, especially pp. 9–10 for the intensity of zeal on behalf of Richard.

with hesitation or compromise or 'non-provens', but believes in heroes like Richard III and villains like Henry VII and Cardinal Morton and perhaps even St Thomas More.*

At the time of the controversy between Gairdner and Markham, academic opinion on the whole was on the side of Gairdner, especially as on points of detail and knowledge of the period he showed himself so much better equipped than his opponent.[51] Since his time most academic historians have lost his faith in the value of the Tudor historical tradition as a guide to the problem. A few like Sir Keith Feiling, and Dr A. L. Rowse, may retain the old robust belief in Richard's villainy and say, as Keith Feiling did, that the Plantagenets came from the devil and 'to the devil they returned in Richard III'.[52] Most academic historians, however, like Professor Kendall or Professor Jacob, are more sympathetic to Richard and more inclined to see the complexity of his character and career. Our generation is more aware of the gaps and ambiguities in the evidence, of the difficulties of making simple judgements on characters. It is symptomatic of the change of atmosphere that Lord Acton could look forward to the first edition of the *Cambridge Modern History* as a great step forward to the day when all European history would have been surveyed and evaluated; whereas in the preface to the second edition Sir George Clark could feel the need to occupy several pages in a discussion of what precisely are historical facts, and the writing of history.[53] And so most academic historians of our time see Richard as a well-intentioned and capable man, who was led by impulse and by circumstance into a hasty usurpation that might have succeeded but happened to be disastrous; and they are more aware than most historians of previous generations writing on this theme how much there is that can never be known for certain.

I undertook this survey to see how far historians have

* Markham had attributed More's History to Cardinal Morton (*Richard III*, p. 169): Miss Tey cast doubt on the *bona fides* of Sir Thomas More himself.

been influenced by the climate of opinion of their time. It is, I think, clear that they have on the whole in fact been influenced a good deal. Must we go further and say that they have in fact been conditioned by it? There are, it seems to me, at least two pieces of evidence against such a determinist view. One is that in every century there were individual historians who refused to conform to pattern. Hume and Lingard were resolutely opposed to Richard when their contemporaries were not; Buc and Markham were equally isolated on the other side; Gairdner was guided by tradition in an era of consciously factual historiography. In other ways, the historian's mind is in the final analysis unpredictable. Lingard the Roman Catholic and Gairdner the Anglo-Catholic accepted the Tudor saga; but so did Hume, the sceptic, whereas Carte, the Jacobite high churchman, did not. Markham and Walpole, striking defenders of Richard III, were amateurs; but so were Hume and Lemon, striking opponents. Generalized arguments are true up to a point and may indicate probabilities; but it is impossible to explain completely why a historian thinks as he does. The mystery of human personality remains.

As for the truth of the matter, there is not only the factor that we do not have enough evidence to be conclusive and probably never shall. There is also the factor that Shakespeare's spell ensures the immortality of the hostile Tudor tradition; it probably also ensures that someone will always be kindly disposed towards the last Plantagenet king. The final truth may always elude us; but that will not prevent inveterate questers from 'still nursing the unconquerable hope, still clutching the inviolable shade'.

NOTES

1. A paper read to the Anglo-American Conference of Historians in London, 14 July 1967, was published in *History* iii, 181 and 202, by kind permission of the Editor.
2. I should like to acknowledge here the stimulus I derived from my discussions on this subject with my friend and former pupil, Mr K. A.

Heathcote, who at my suggestion wrote in 1952 a thesis on the historiography of Richard III for the Honours History B.A. Degree of the University of Liverpool.

3. Max Buedinger, 'König Richard III von England', *Sammlung wissenschaftlicher Vorträge zu Wien* (1858), 37.

4. See Sir Harold Nicolson's review of Professor P. M. Kendall's *Richard III* in *The Observer*, 1 January 1956.

5. Probably the most useful of these investigations is still G. B. Churchill's *Richard III up to Shakepeare*, a study of nearly 550 pages made for the Ph.D. degree of the University of Berlin in 1900.

6. *The Constitutional History of England*, vol 3, 5th ed., 1896, p. 232.

7. Churchill, *op. cit.*, pp. 118–19. For an interesting recent analysis of Sir Thomas More's *History of King Richard III*, see R. S. Sylvester's edition (1963); though Professor Sylvester fails to realize (p. lxxx) that the sixteenth century did not distinguish clearly between 'history' in our sense and history in the meaning of 'story' or 'drama'.

8. Of the many books that examine the sources of the Elizabethan pattern of a moral sequence in history, one of the most useful is I. Ribner, *The English history play in the age of Shakespeare* (1957).

9. E. W. M. Tillyard, *Shakespeare's History Plays* (1948), p. 48.

10. *History of the World* (1614), Preface, p. 10.

11. *Ibid.*, pp. 7, 8, 11.

12. F. Bacon, *The History of the Reign of King Henry VII*, 1622; W. Habington, *The Reign of King Edward IV*, 1640; W. Camden, *Britannia*, ed. R. Gough, 4 vols., 1806, I. 386.

13. *The Life and Reign of Richard III*, in W. Kennett's *Complete History of England*, 3 vols., ed. 1706, I. 514–16.

14. *Ibid.*, I. 566.

15. *Ibid.*, I. 548, 549.

16. W. Prynne, *King Richard the Third Revived* (1656).

17. This tract is followed in the British Museum volume by two tracts entitled *Monumentum Regale, or a Tombe erected for that incomparable and glorious Monarch, Charles the First* (1649), and *A Deep Groan Fetch'd at the Funerall of that incomparable and glorious Monarch Charles the First* (1649).

18. E.g. *A letter from a Gentleman of Quality . . . shewing how improbable (if not impossible) it is to Bar the next Heir in the Right Line from the Succession* (1679).

19. See *D.N.B.* and E. Fueter, *Histoire de l'Historiographie Moderne*, 1914, pp. 397–9.

20. Paul de Rapin de Thoyras, *History of England*, ed. N. Tindal, 1732–3, I. Introduction, p. iv.

21. Paul de Rapin de Thoyras, *History of England*, I. 615, 647.

22. T. Carte, *A General History of England*, 4 vols., 1747–55.

23. D. Hume, *History of England*, ed. T. Smollett, 1825, 3. 281.

24. 'Hume and his Influence upon History', *Quarterly Review*, 1843–44, 554.

25. For Lord Macaulay's searing attack on Hume's methods as a historian, see J. W. Thompson, *A History of Historical Writing*, 1942, II, 71.

26. R. W. Ketton-Cremer, *Horace Walpole*, 1940, p. 23.

27. *Horace Walpole's Correspondence with George Selwyn, Lord Lincoln, etc.*, ed. W. S. Lewis and R. A. Smith, 1961, pp. 125–7.

44 THE TUDORS

28. Guthrie wrote (anonymously) in the *Critical Review*, XXV, 116–25; F. G. G(uy-dickens) of the Middle Temple, *An answer to Mr. Horace Walpole's late work*, 1768; E. Gibbon, *Miscellaneous Works*, ed. Lord Sheffield, 1814, 3. 331–49.

29. Dr Milles read to the Antiquaries a compte-rendu which was printed in *Archaeologia*, I (1770), pp. 361–83; Robert Masters read another critical paper which was printed in *Archaeologia*, II (1771), pp. 189–215.

30. W. Hutton, *The Battle of Bosworth Field*, 1788; E. Spelman and G. W. Lemon, *The History of the Civil Wars between York and Lancaster, comprehending the Lives of Edward IV and his brother Richard III*, 1792; R. Henry, *History of Great Britain*, extended by M. Laing, 1793.

31. Henry, *op. cit.*, 5th edn., 1814, XII, p. 413.

32. *Lord Orford's Works*, 1798, II. 251*–252*.

33. Sharon Turner, *Richard the Third, A Poem*, 1845, pp. iii–iv.

34. *Ibid.*, p. vi.

35. *The History of England during the Middle Ages*, 3rd edn., 1830, III. 530.

36. Turner, *History of England during the Middle Ages*, III. 423.

37. *Ibid.*, p. 506.

38. N. H. Nicolas, *Privy Expenses of Elizabeth of York and Wardrobe Accounts of Edward the Fourth*, 1830, pp. iv–xiv.

39. C. A. Halsted, *Richard III as Duke of Gloucester and King of England* (2 vols., 1844); J. H. Jesse, *Memoirs of King Richard III* (1862).

40. Halsted, *op. cit.*, I, 123, II, 21.

41. Similarly, C. Wessel, *Richard III in Shakespeare's plays compared with Richard III in history* (Eschwege, 1876) contrasts the two characters, and follows in the main Sharon Turner's view.

42. Cf. *Letters and Papers, etc.*, I. xv–xx and II. xv–xviii.

43. J. Gairdner, *History of the Life and Reign of Richard the Third*, revised edn., 1898, p. xi.

44. *Ibid.*, p. 13.

45. A. O. Legge, *The Unpopular King*, 2 vols., 1885.

46. Cf. Sir Albert H. Markham, *The Life of Sir Clements R. Markham*, 1917, Appendix B, pp. 366–8.

47. *Ibid.*, p. 298.

48. C. R. Markham, *op. cit.*, pp. 210–16.

49. C. R. Markham, *op. cit.*, p. 156. Cf. the extremely eulogistic summary of Richard's character, pp. 159–64.

50. C. R. Markham, *King Edward VI*, 1907, p. 3.

51. See, for example, the debate between them in *E.H.R.*, VI (1891).

52. K. Feiling, *A History of England*, 1950, p. 313.

53. *Cambridge Historical Journal*, VIII (1945), 57 ff.; *The New Cambridge Modern History*, vol. I, 1957, pp. xxv ff.

PART TWO

Henry VIII

HENRY VIII

by

G. R. ELTON

What shall we think of Henry VIII? However that question
has been or may be answered, one reply is apparently
impossible. Not even the most resolute believer in deterministic
interpretations of history seems able to escape the spell of that
magnificent figure; I know of no book on the age which does not
allow the king a place somewhere at least near the centre of
the stage. It is therefore self-evident that what one thinks of
Henry VIII is an entirely fundamental part of what one thinks of
sixteenth-century England; no one can arrive at a sensible
view of that period without making for himself a convincingly
real picture of the King. At first glance, this might seem no
difficult task. No king of England is more familiar to his
countrymen; indeed, he is the only one whose portrait the vast
majority would recognize on sight. They know one fact about
quite a few other sovereigns. Charles I lost his head, Charles
II had Nell Gwyn, George III went mad. Of Henry VIII
they know two things: he made the Reformation, and he had
six wives. Even if only the second fact is beyond dispute, there
is something oddly adequate about this body of knowledge.
Henry's fame rests on a striking personality, expressing itself
in his technicoloured private life, and on the almost perfect
success of his sovereign policy. The King stamped himself on
his age and country with all the vehemence of the true ruler;
today he appears as the very embodiment of personal monarchy.
Any study of Henry VIII is indeed a study in the nature of
personal monarchy, but that concept is not precise. It means
different things in different hands, and some error has arisen
from the supposition that if Henry VIII was a true personal

monarch, he must in consequence have been the maker and deviser of all that happened in his day.

In periods of patchy evidence, it is always difficult to ascribe responsibility and assess originality, so that one tends to use the name of the nominal ruler as a symbol for the multitude of men who go to make up the government of a country over a number of years. When the nominal ruler is so fiercely evident, leaves so profound and prolonged an impression, and looks so much a king *par excellence*, it seems clearly sensible to suppose that the symbol stands for the reality. Froude came to the study of the reign with every ingrained prejudice against that bloodstained monster, Henry VIII; he left it with an ardent admiration for the King.[1] A. F. Pollard, sound Victorian liberal though he was, gave the King not only the respect of the historian but also the worship of the devotee.[2] 'The most remarkable man who ever sat on the English throne'; 'it was the King and the King alone, who kept England on the course he had mapped out'; such phrases take some justifying. Of course, they are supposed to arise from a dispassionate study of the evidence, but they go beyond the mere analysis of the King's doings to an almost bemused delight in what he is thought to have done. In this they perhaps represent only the feelings of the stalwart Protestant; but it is more to the point that this approval of the Reformation should have become so firmly attached to a monarch whom Pollard, at least, believed never to have wavered from doctrinal orthodoxy.

Anyone who wants to take an independent look at Henry VIII is bound to come up against Pollard whose splendidly executed portrait (not a Holbein, but neither a Sargent – perhaps a Winterhalter?) has called the field for nearly sixty years. Indeed, except for one or two popular but negligible book,[3] no further biography has even appeared since 1902.[4] What may perhaps be called a Catholic revival in historical writing, together with the experiences of the last generation, have here and there produced attacks on this figure inherited

from a pleasanter age. It has become customary to trace the
easy parallels between the sixteenth and twentieth centuries,
with their ideological wars, state trials, subversive movements
and all the rest; and even if that endeavour has on occasion led
to some striking historical misjudgements, it has produced a
drop in Henry's stock.* At least we are no longer quite so likely
to accept Henry's egomania with indulgence merely because
it somehow helped to advance the cause of Protestant England;
recognizing his mixture of brutal will and cunning skill for what
it was, we shall not so readily submerge the nastiness of the
man in approval of the achievement. When Pollard roundly
asserted that Henry was never capable of 'a lust for superfluous
butchery',[5] we must wonder where for him superfluity had
its beginning. Even the romantic view of the King, playing
up his film-star and football-hero qualities in precisely the way
that appealed to his own subjects, is constrained to take note
of what is then called his 'darker' or 'satanic' side.[6] All these
minor adjustments, all these revulsions of taste, do not, however, take away from the granite core of Pollard's Henry VIII,
the King who 'surrounded by faint hearts and fearful minds
... neither faltered nor failed', the pilot who weathered the
storm. Inevitably, if one is to arrive at a reasoned view of
Henry VIII's place in history, one must first consider Pollard's
view and assess its validity.

* * *

In Pollard's eyes, Henry VIII was essentially a simple man,
despite his secret counsels and careful ways. A king at eighteen,
a young athlete but also an intellectual, he was content to enjoy
life in a variety of ways and left business to others. From 1514
to 1529 he allowed Wolsey to govern, though he never entirely
abdicated his place to the Cardinal. He matured slowly, but by
1529, when Wolsey failed in the matter of the Divorce, he was

---

* When some years ago Mr A. J. P. Taylor likened Tito's quarrel with
Moscow to Henry VIII's break with Rome, it was uncertain which was
the more striking – the immediate appositeness or the ultimate nullity of
the comparison.

ready to take over. (In passing, it may be noted that a Tudor who did not 'mature' till he was thirty-eight arouses one's scepticism.) From then onwards, he remained his own prime minister, and the remainder of the reign witnessed a series of successful actions elevating both his monarchy and the nation's independence and power to new heights. For Pollard the reign therefore fell into two parts: the years during which Henry 'had been kept in leading strings by Wolsey's and other clerical influences', on the one hand; on the other, the later years during which he first consolidated his personal supremacy in England and then extended it over the rest of the British Isles.[7]

For this notion of a quite straightforward course of development, determined and guided by the growth of one particular personality, Pollard offered no evidence except a story so slanted as to support the interpretation. He never argued his case; he assumed it. Yet any critical consideration of it at once discovers a number of manifest difficulties. Even if one is to accept without question his account of the Wolsey era, can one really see a perfect unity in the years 1529–47? Pollard seems to maintain not only that the pointless French war of 1542–4 was wise policy, but also that Henry's attack on Scottish independence in 1545–6 was sensible and constructive, though in the face of Henry's manifest failure to rivet English rule on Scotland even he was compelled to suggest some tentative criticisms.[8] Of the policy in general, however, he approves, arguing that in this last war Henry was not pursuing the 'Wolsey policy' of mere glory and aggrandizement but had in mind the menace of a personal union between France and Scotland. We look in vain beyond the assertion for the proof, and we cannot forget that the whole threat of a Franco-Scottish union neither did nor could begin to show until after Solway Moss, the death of James V, and the growingly palpable danger of an English conquest of Scotland.

In fact, without at this stage committing oneself to any explanation, one cannot but be immediately struck by the marked differences in purpose and success that marked the

1530s and 1540s, by the contrast between the highly successful internal policy in the first decade and the fumblingly unsuccessful external policy of the second. Moreover, the latter even threatened much of the internal achievement of the former: it aggravated, if it did not call forth, the great economic crisis. The truth about that period of inflation and distress was only partially known when Pollard wrote, though it must be said that even what he could have known ought to have influenced his account a good deal more than it did. In his book on Henry VIII he does not mention debasement and has nothing to say on inflation. Thus, even if one were to agree that the years from Wolsey's fall to the dissolution of the Reformation Parliament saw a continuous policy inspired by one man (and I have shown elsewhere why I should stress the changes brought about by Thomas Cromwell's arrival in power in 1531–2),[9] it is quite impossible to overlook a drastic change for the worse in 1541–2, when the King resumed the policy of continental alliances and military enterprises.* Either Henry VIII was not the unfailing political genius of Pollard's imagining, or the policy of the second half of his reign was not so exclusively dominated by one man. Or, for that matter, both these points may be true.

A few particular pieces of Pollard's picture may be subjected to closer analysis, in order to show the slender grounds on which some apparently well-founded parts of it rest. It is essential to his view that Henry should be seen as 'innocent', idealistic, and trusting in his early years – a lamb going to slaughter among the wolves of the international scene, and a Prince Charming at home. Then we are shown the lamb learning its lesson and Prince Charming gradually losing his bloom; we are back with a Henry VIII slowly maturing – in

* Pollard maintained (*Henry VIII*, pp. 149 f.) that after 1529 Henry avoided a spirited foreign policy. This is true down to the early forties, and certainly Wolsey was largely responsible for the concentration on foreign policy which marked the years 1515–28. But to see in the wars after 1541 nothing but a sensible policy for the consolidation of 'Great Britain' is surely to misread the situation.

cask, as it were. Of course, there is some truth in this; all men grow older and intelligent men learn from experience. No one doubts that advancing years and increasing ill-health left their mark on Henry VIII. Unquestionably, his physical grossness, suspicious arrogance and political dexterity all grew more marked as self-indulgence and the effects of adulation worked on one of the most purely egotistic temperaments known to history. What is less clear is whether Henry was really so innocent in his youth – so very different in essentials (allowing for differences in degree) from what later years showed him to be. It was in 1516, when twenty-five years old, that he expressed his view of his kingship as 'having no superior on earth'; as far as his belief in his own exalted position went, greater age and experience could not enlarge an assurance already complete. Pollard glides easily over the executions of Empson and Dudley, arranged on manifestly false charges of treason and sacrificed to the demands of popularity. It may well be that the idea came from Henry's ministers; but the whole episode carries all the stigmata of political motive, sickening self-righteousness and drastic success which mark later occasions in the reign when others whose services had become inconvenient (Anne Boleyn, Cromwell, the Howards) found themselves in the same unhappy position. It is really very difficult to believe that even the adolescent Henry VIII was not fully conversant with the use of managed state trials.

More dubious still is Pollard's notion that the trusting idealist was horribly deceived and exploited by his wicked allies in the war of 1512–14. He tells the story exclusively from the calendar of *Letters and Papers of the Reign of Henry VIII*,[10] and although that collection includes some material from continental archives, a less insular body of evidence would surely cast a different light. This is the more certain because Pollard's version does not really hold together. Henry, we are told, entered the war purely because of his zeal for the church. He was then time and again deceived by Ferdinand the Catholic and the Emperor Maximilian, though for long he refused to credit their duplicity and remained eager only to help the Pope. It thus comes as something of a surprise to find the story end with the lamb's unheralded triumph over the wolves: 'Maximilian and Ferdinand were left out in the cold'. The upshot of all those manoeuvres was England's marriage alliance with the common enemy, France, a manifest victory for Henry. That Ferdinand and Maximilian behaved badly and tortuously is unquestionably true; but the fact that only Henry got positive advantages (including money and territory) does make one wonder about his innocence and idealism. It would surely be a simpler and more probable view which saw his political abilities and understanding as highly developed even at this stage and took a less patriotically trusting line over his frequent protestations of noble intentions and gentlemanly instincts. In brief, Pollard's view fails to convince me because it essentially assumes a unity in the reign created by the dominance of the King's person and action, and then explains the obvious differences of its parts (reduced beyond the facts) by postulating unacceptably profound differences between the King's youth and manhood and age. Henry changed as all men change, but (like most men) he did so within clearly defined limits of character, intellect and purpose which are discernible from the first. In consequence, the changing character of the reign – the contrasts both in what was done and how it was done – cannot be explained by looking only at him.

There are also indications that the picture painted by Pollard, and very generally accepted, of a man sovereignly in control of all that went on, cannot be altogether true. Take the case of his ministers. Certainly, both Wolsey and Cromwell fell only because the King abandoned them: he made them, he maintained them, he alone could destroy them. Yet he regretted their loss soon after and recognized that he had been inveigled into a false step. He kept the possibility of recalling Wolsey in mind – to such good effect that Norfolk and the Council found it necessary to get evidence of the Cardinal's continued political activity and be rid of him that way. In Cromwell's case, Henry frankly admitted the truth when he complained that his other councillors had, 'upon light pretexts, by false accusations . . . made him put to death the most faithful servant he ever had'.[11] This was exactly what had happened;[12] and it underlines the relative ease with which this powerful and personal monarch could be manipulated by those who knew how to play on his prejudices, fears and suspicions. Historians for ever quote Sir Thomas More's remark to Cromwell that if the lion but knew his own strength it were hard for anyone to hold him; but they do not seem to realize that this sufficiently penetrating (if also sufficiently obvious) insight both underestimated the lion's self-knowledge from the start and proves nothing about his readiness to be tricked by others into the use of his strength. Why, even in the most personal matter of all, Henry was easily enough caught in webs spun by the manipulators. A man who marries six wives is not a man who perfectly controls his own fate; and twice at least he married in obedience to other people's management. The Howards yoked him to his second Catherine as surely as Cromwell, more openly, forced his second Anne upon him.

*   *   *

All this is not intended in the least to deny Henry's very real abilities, but only to suggest that we surely cannot accept an argument unsupported by evidence which ascribes to him alone the mastery of events, the making of policy, and the detailed and specific government of the country. Personal monarchy does not necessarily require any of this. It is enough if the monarch observes the two essentials of such a form of kingship, as Henry VIII unquestionably did: he always and fully represented its symbolic side, and he always remained the last and ultimately decisive factor in government. The first point must be seen in its proper importance. Used as we are to a monarchy for long described, rather patronizingly, as a symbolic figurehead, we may easily overlook the vital necessity and great political strength in the sixteenth century of a king who was visibly king and head of the nation. Although it is not true, as has sometimes been alleged, that the Tudor age could not make a distinction between the Crown and its holder, it remains true that ordinarily it preferred not to have to make the distinction. However much we may talk of an age of nationalism and similar abstractions, the fact that allegiance was given to an embodied head, to the person of the king in the most literal way, is very plain. This semi-divine king, both distant and near – for privacy was a thing barely known to kings – not only stood for the nation and the commonwealth, symbolizing something else, but himself demanded and received a personal and direct devotion which during the stresses of the Reformation came at times very near idolatry. In its most restricted sense, personal monarchy perhaps reached its apogee in Henry VIII. At this task of personal projection he was better than his father, who had been a better and abler king; more successful even than his daughter, who died with court and country emerging from the spell she had cast. No matter what he did, Henry VIII never experienced any weakening in the personal magnetism which worked upon all sorts and conditions of men. From the day that he ascended the throne, so full of the Renaissance virtues that for once the panegyrists could mean what they said, to the day thirty-eight years later when the swollen wreck of a fine body at last released the indomitable spirit, the King stood in the world's eye as the true figure of all that kingship meant. Body and mind equipped him better for this than either Charles V or Francis I, both politically more powerful in fact. No person was ever more monarchical, no monarchy more personal in this sense, than Henry VIII's.

Nor, of course, was it all show. He ruled as well as reigned; no man ever dominated Henry VIII, and few could keep even a guiding hand on him for long. During Wolsey's ascendancy he seemed at times to retire from the political scene. But even though he allowed the Cardinal to run things (till Wolsey himself came to believe in the implications of that dangerous cognomen, *alter rex*), he asserted himself at times, and always with contemptuous ease. As early as 1516, when he was still in the main preoccupied with his intellectual, athletic and amatory amusements, he taught Wolsey a lesson by compelling him to seek pardon on his knees in the clergy's quarrel with the laity which arose out of Richard Hunne's case. Attempts to investigate and improve the machinery of government were undertaken in 1518–19 and 1526, in response to the King's demands for greater efficiency and influence; the fact that nothing came of them reflects on both King and minister, but it does not permit us to overlook Henry's very evident activity in government even at this stage. The correspondence of those years provides plenty of evidence of his constant concern with affairs: he had, for instance, his own view on the government of Ireland.[13] He let Wolsey govern and often gave him a free hand; but he never ceased to insert himself at intervals into the process by which policy came to be both devised and executed.

If Wolsey was arrogant, he yet showed a proper deference to the King; while he deceived himself into thinking that the reality of power lay with him, he yet accorded Henry some of the show. Cromwell, who never reached Wolsey's position in the world, or his income, and who took little stock in the trappings of glory, went much further in submission. Self-reliant and sturdy towards all others, he adopted towards Henry a fulsomeness of tone, a depth of courtier-like phraseology, for which historians (who often, in their own way and without Cromwell's compelling reasons, are quite as much awed by the King) have never forgiven him. The difference did not entirely lie in the ministers; unquestionably the Divorce and the political complications which ensued changed Henry's habits. Immediately after Wolsey's fall he had no single minister to govern for him, and he therefore necessarily devoted more of his time and thought to affairs than before. Not vastly more: there was no change, however gradual, from playboy to statesman, for he had never really been the first and was never really to be the second. But he certainly demonstrated his personal control more deliberately. He began to see foreign ambassadors more often himself, even though the meetings in which the real negotiations were carried on continued to take place with his ministers. He never attended Council meetings, a reasonable practice also followed by Elizabeth; but he now saw to it that Council discussions were not the sham of Wolsey's day and that he was given advice, not information on action taken. He read state papers and occasionally corrected them. To the superficial eye he was very much in charge, an appearance corroborated by Cromwell's careful language and willingness to let all things appear to have come from him. Cromwell was always using 'his highness' pleasure' in his letters and instructions; it was always 'the king so wills it' or 'his grace commandeth me to say', though there is plenty of evidence (including some of the charges levelled against him in his attainder) that these phrases did not necessarily mean that Henry had even heard of the case in question. Anyone who has ever received a letter on some minor point from some underling in a ministry, beginning 'I am instructed by Her Majesty's Secretary of State', will perhaps be able to put a more intelligent than literal interpretation on such words.

Still, it all goes to show what no one then doubted, as no one need doubt it now: no matter what was decided, the last word remained with the king. Cromwell's fall, more dramatically sudden than Wolsey's, underlined this, and Henry thereafter thought himself well able to govern without any chief minister. It is sometimes argued that his experience with Wolsey and Cromwell taught him the unwisdom of concentrating so much power in one hand, and I am far from denying the pathological suspiciousness which grew upon him with increasing age, ill health, and success. But I find it impossible to believe that he ever thought himself even remotely unable to do as he pleased with any of his servants. Not fear of over-

mighty subjects, but the absence of any obvious successor to
Cromwell, the existence of two religious factions and mis-
placed confidence in his own powers led Henry VIII to do
without a single leading minister after 1540. Those were also
the only years in his reign when government policy was directly
disastrous to the country.

In one kind of business Henry seems always to have been
the decisive factor from beginning to end – in the business,
that is, of political trials and the persecution of important individuals. It is possible that the Duke of Buckingham suffered
because Wolsey tricked the King into suspicion, and
Cromwell may have worked off a personal animus against the
Poles. But even these cases are dubious, and in such other in-
stances as Empson and Dudley, More and Fisher, Anne Boleyn
and the Earl of Surrey, not to mention Wolsey and Cromwell
themselves, the real blood-guilt lies with the King. Time and
again, real viciousness palpably enters these cases only with
his personal participation. Faction strife and personal ambition
brought their grim battles, but it was the King's hand that
held the axe. Everybody accepted the fact and the supposed
necessity of these 'prepared' trials with their edifying scaffold-
scenes, but only the King gives the impression of believing in
them, sincere horror of the alleged deed mingling in him with
an unrelenting thirst for revenge. Cromwell treated More with
compassion and respect until he had a word from on high. In
1536, when Cromwell tried to protect the freshly cowed Car-
thusians against the royal desire to expel them from their house,
he earned a severe reprimand: in Henry's view, their late submission could not wipe out the guilt of their long resistance.
Nor did Cromwell's attempts in 1537 to secure some sort of
relief for the relatives of those 'who have suffered' (those
hanged for taking part in the northern rising) ever result in
action from the King.[14] The Countess of Salisbury lived while
Cromwell lived, though under sentence of death; it was Henry
who, by carrying out this sentence, had the old lady callously
disposed of in 1541. The clearing of the Tower in that year,

which to Pollard is evidence of a deteriorating character,[15] is after all matched by a similar step during the early and allegedly glorious years when in 1513 the Earl of Suffolk went to the scaffold to secure the home front during the forthcoming war. In a sense, Henry VIII's most horrifying victims were not the often and justly lamented righteous men of the 1530s, but rather the first and last men he attacked: Empson and Dudley in 1509, the Howards in 1546. These victims were unattractive and did not fall for religion's sake, which has obscured the fact that they were unusually innocent of the charges preferred. More and Fisher did stand in the way of a revolution, and were politically dangerous, and Fisher, at any rate, had by any definition dallied with treason; Empson and Dudley were killed to gain popularity and Surrey to satisfy tyrannic suspicion. For these killings, as for the rest, Henry VIII must himself take responsibility, not only because his ultimate power could so easily have stopped them, but because in fact he instigated and drove on the process. This evil readiness to commit political or dynastic murder arose directly from his militant self-righteousness; it was alien both to Wolsey's flamboyant hypocrisy and Cromwell's sardonic realism.

* * *

However, if so much active personal monarchy can be traced in the reign – if Henry was 'a real king' both to the eye and in action – why should one deny his full control of policy and affairs? In what respect is it reasonable to suppose that Pollard's straightforward assumption of Henry's directing hand overestimated his influence and impact? There are two lines of argument which strongly urge one to conclude that, unlike Henry VII or even Elizabeth, Henry VIII was not master or maker of his own fate or that of his country. In the first place, by ignoring the steady hard work of government and relying on ministers to attend to business, he gravely limited the effectiveness of that ultimate control of his. He did not exercise it in either a vacuum or a situation of his own creation, but in

circumstances in which his choice had in great part been pre-
determined by the action of others. Secondly, an analysis of
the reign into its significant periods indicates that Henry relied
on others not only for the day-to-day conduct of affairs but
also for any general or specific ideas in approaching action. He
was an opportunist, an inspired opportunist, making the most
of other men's help in a given situation, rather than a creative
statesman. This might not have limited his personal influence
at most ordinary times, but in a reign which witnessed much
fundamental policy-making – even revolution – Henry's dis-
ability in this respect matters. After all, we are concerned not
with a generalized problem of personal monarchy, but with the
question, for instance, whether it was really the King himself
who devised the policy of the Reformation.

Henry was not an active administrator. From first to last he
seems to have found attention to the details of business a bit
of a bore. In his younger days his secretaries had to catch him
as they could, between his amusements; in particular, there were
many complaints that hunting (a sport, one of them said, which
the King was turning into a martyrdom) interfered with the
despatch of papers. He hated writing letters and never paid
the slightest attention to financial affairs. This last, an understandable enough foible, was to cost him dear towards the end
of his reign. It is true that he commonly saw state papers, or
at least summaries prepared for him, and that diplomatic instructions required his personal signature: once again one must
not exaggerate his relative indolence and reluctance into ineffec-
tualness. It is well known that in his last years, when he was
often ill, many documents requiring his signature were instead
stamped with a facsimile; but it does not appear to be so well
known that the first extant example of a stamped letter occurs
in 1512,* or that throughout the 1530s many important documents, especially warrants for payments, were so authen-
ticated.[16] That in fact it mattered little whether he ever saw

---

* *Letters and Papers*, i. 1217: an order concerning the mustering of
tenants, certainly not a piece of mere administrative routine.

such orders is well illustrated by the regularity with which Cromwell authorized and made payments before obtaining the royal warrants.[17] Even in foreign affairs, where the King assuredly kept a closer watch, he relied for information on abstracts and for his own letters on drafts prepared by his ministers. Very few such drafts bear corrections in his own hand, a fact which reflects on an anecdote recorded in Elizabeth's reign. It is reported that when Sir William Petre, on being appointed principal secretary (1544), showed his dismay at the way in which Henry 'crossed and blotted out many things in a writing which he had made', he was told not to take it to heart: 'for it is I,' said the King, 'who made Cromwell, Wriothesley and Paget good secretaries, and so must I do to thee'.[18] The story may well be true; by 1544 Henry may well have persuaded himself that things had happened thus. In fact, there is no sign in the many drafts which Cromwell and Wriothesley prepared for him that he had anything to teach them. The true position was perhaps better described in an aside of Sir Francis Bryan's when on embassy to France: 'In the King's letters,' he told Cromwell, 'you touched the quick.' Henry's agents knew who wrote his letters.[19]

Nor is there, in general, any notable difference in these working habits at different times. Both as a young and as an old king, Henry concerned himself with dispatches, accepted drafts, demanded changes. The evidence is too bulky to be detailed here and too patchy for any statistical assessment. If one may go by impressions, one must say that Henry probably saw more letters and papers during Cromwell's ascendancy, but exercised a more evident initiative in government during Wolsey's. While he pressed the Cardinal several times to undertake reforms of the administration,[20] he never played any part in the many such reforms carried out by the lord privy seal.[21] He never interfered with Cromwell's financial arrangements as he did with Wolsey's when in 1518 he insisted on supervising the payment of certain ambassadors' charges;[22] it is instructive to compare his intervention in the election at Wilton Nunnery in

1528 with his total ignorance of the abbatial election at Rievaulx in 1533.[23] On the other hand, he never told anyone to treat Cromwell's letters as though they came from himself, as in 1517 he told Ghinucci to treat Wolsey's.[24] Though throughout his reign Henry kept an eye on some details and dealt with some business, he never did enough of this either before or after 1529 to save himself from having to follow the lead given by his ministers. There was, of course, no reason why he should. He delegated power in the confidence that he could rely on his advisers and agents; he knew he could always discard the policy with the minister if he wished to do so. His attitude to business shows that he was wise enough to realize that there are other things in life. But the evidence is strong that while a minister held power it was he and not the King who controlled and devised policy.

Of course, the objection to this argument from the papers is that the King need not have left any visible evidence of his personal activity in the record. What was to prevent him instructing his ministers to draw up documents of a given tenor or even dictating them, so that what appeared as the work of a servant was really the King's own? This objection, which – since we have no knowledge of conversations held – can never be altogether controverted, is yet seriously weakened by several facts. On the one occasion (in 1521) when we are explicitly told that the King dictated a dispatch, the matter is treated as entirely out of the ordinary, requiring detailed description.[25] In the 1530s it is pretty clear that Henry did not dictate his letters which were usually written away from court, commonly in Cromwell's private office. Under Wolsey, when diplomatic negotiations were often carried on without the King being aware of any details, the point is even plainer. There is also plenty of evidence that such matters as he did study had as a rule got very near to their final stage before he had a chance of affecting them. And lastly, the argument that the absence of Henry's handwriting from the papers proves little would be stronger if the King had not on occasion taken the trouble to correct what was put before him. Significantly, his hand occurs most frequently on papers with a theological or ecclesiastical import. These aroused his intellectual interest as well as his private preoccupations, and he was thus willing to amend drafts of the Act of Six Articles or scribble comments in the margins of argumentative letters concerning his supremacy in the church. The total of such corrections is not large, but there is enough to give some support for the view that absence of corrections – and the presence of corrections by others – argues absence of significant influence. The most striking example of all occurs in the preparation of the Act against Appeals to Rome (1533), which not only cost much labour but was also so central to the whole development of the Reformation that, if indeed it was Henry who thought up the policy and principles of that revolution, one would expect to find him actively participating in this if nothing else. There are eight surviving drafts of this statute, nearly all of them plentifully corrected, mostly by Cromwell. But the King, too, let his hand appear: on one draft he made a few minor corrections by addition and excision, some of which disappeared again at a later stage.[26] No one wants to argue that Henry did not know what was going on or fully authorize the policy embodied in this act and others; but it is apparent that there is no reason at all for supposing that his own mind was behind these measures and very good reason for supposing that it was not.

*   *   *

The evidence of the record is therefore quite definitely that the King more often than not simply accepted and endorsed policies and measures which he did not initiate. His was the activating force in an engine whose design owed most to other brains and hands. Documentary evidence is doubtless not the whole of history, but arguments relying on its neglect are surely neither here nor there. If the record tells the truth, one would expect the reign to show changing characteristics as ministers changed. And this indeed is what we find. The reign consists essentially

of three periods: Wolsey's ascendancy, which was marked by
an over-riding concern with foreign affairs and at home by
the expansion of conciliar jurisdiction; Cromwell's years of
power when the government was mainly occupied with the
church and the royal supremacy, with administrative and social
reform, with finance, the use of Parliament and the recovery
of common-law ascendancy; and the last seven years, which
ought to have been devoted primarily to the settlement of the
religious question but were in fact bedevilled by war and economic crisis. Two brief periods (1509–12 and 1529–31) precede
the arrival in power of the two great ministers and have no
discernible character of their own, except perhaps ineffectual-
ness. These different preoccupations are in themselves interesting enough, but more striking still are the unmistakable differences in mood, temper, method and attitude to business. The
Wolsey period was one of outward glory, much ostentation and
exuberance, so much so that some historians – not all of them
necessarily hostile to the Reformation – have been willing to
see in 1530 the end of the really important and fruitful period
of Henry's reign. The years of Cromwell's ministry give an
impression of singular and relentless purpose, of ends achieved
without fuss but with incisive assurance. The keynote of the last
years is a frustrating devotion to opportunism – an uneasy
tinkering with the great internal problem, unity in religion, combined with a reckless and once again unsuccessful foreign policy.

Now it has been objected, sensibly enough, that these differences merely reflect differences in problems and circumstances to which Henry reacted at need.[27] One can suppose him
engaged in diplomatic and warlike games at a time when
England's puny strength could make itself felt in a Europe still
fairly balanced between the powers of France and Spain, until
the virtual triumph of Charles V in 1525–8 rendered such
pretensions futile. One may well agree that the Divorce and the
break with Rome involved so many internal problems that
Henry naturally abandoned Europe and concentrated on re-
organizing his realm. One might even see some point in the

argument that the end of Cromwell coincided with the King's realization that he was now internally secure and with the renewal of conflict between Charles V and Francis I: once again he was free to engage in large foreign ambitions. With greater reluctance still (and little respect for the facts) one might even be prepared to argue that the troubles of the 1540s were due to deteriorating economic circumstances, to inflation and other impersonal factors. A case of sorts can be made for seeing in the periods of the reign nothing more than the changing interests and capacities of one man, and Pollard so explained them in his idiosyncratic picture of Henry VIII 'maturing' in his late thirties.

Yet it will not do. Quite apart from the fact that Pollard's approach does not explain the very great changes in 'atmosphere' as distinct from things done, some of these arguments are plainly false. It was not changing circumstances but impatience, over-confidence, and folly which turned policy after 1540 from internal to external preoccupations. The death of Cromwell did not coincide with an end to the sort of problems that he had given his first attention to. The troubles of 1544–6, including the inflation, resulted in great part directly from the King's warlike policy. If Henry, as it is often put, learned from Wolsey the folly of foreign entanglements, why did he resume war and entanglements in 1541? Why was the period of Cromwell's ascendancy the only one during which war would have seemed reasonable, because defensive, but never happened? Why was England totally neutral in only one of the Habsburg-Valois conflicts of the time, that of 1536–8? We are sometimes assured that the great administrative reforms of the 1530s were forced on the government by the ecclesiastical upheavals and political reconstruction of that decade. But this ignores the facts that administrative reform had been plainly necessary since Henry VII's death, that Wolsey at least twice contemplated but avoided reforms which would have weakened his personal control, and that many of Cromwell's measures answered perennial, not new, problems. Such problems as were new had been in great part created by the revolutionary measures of the government associated with Cromwell. Henry's own mind did not develop so as to explain the changes. He thought himself subject to no other power on earth both in 1516 and in 1534; but in 1521 he showed, by ascribing to the Pope powers which even Thomas More thought excessive, that it would be quite wrong to deduce from this that he himself developed the notion of a royal supremacy in the church. I have shown elsewhere that the contrasting policies towards Rome in 1529–31 (unimaginative, bombastic, sterile) and 1532–4 (direct, simple, successful) cannot be explained on the supposition that they were both inspired by the King.[28] A general air of vigour and powerful life may well be seen emanating from Henry throughout his reign; the specific work of government, the ideas underlying it, and the policies put into effect at different times varied as Henry's ministers took over from one another. The genuine and increasing difficulties of the last seven years, most of them traceable to some particular error of policy at a time when Henry did without the support of a single strong hand and is most likely to have been in direct control himself, underline the quality of his own mind. He was no statesman, and inasmuch as qualities of statesmanship can be discerned in his reign they must be looked for elsewhere.

This absence of truly analytical and constructive abilities is also suggested by what we know of Henry's intellectual equipment. That he was intelligent is not in doubt: he had a very good brain. He could read men and pick men, no one better. His political understanding of what was within and what outside his powers practically never failed him. Perhaps this last quality, so surprisingly unaffected by the flowering of a native egoism nourished by adulation, is the hallmark of his particular genius: if he never failed in anything he attempted, it was because he never attempted anything in which he could not succeed. His judgement of this delicate dividing line was nearly unerring. In consequence he not only left the world gasping, but – to note it in passing – got his way like a despot without

3—TT • •

ever ruling despotically, ignoring the law, or stifling opposition in Council or Parliament. However, his upbringing had given his intelligence an interest in things intellectual, and the events of his reign (especially the break with Rome) raised fundamental intellectual, even academic, issues to a level of first importance in politics. It cannot be said that the questions asked by events found a perfect answer from the King. His own pronouncements on theory are mostly conventional or even platitudinous (though well expressed), like his book against Luther or his speech on religious unity to the 1545 Parliament.[29] When he tried his hand at a piece of political theory, he relied on something told him by his judges and was liable to get muddled in the process.[30] Thomas Starkey's *Exhortation to the People*, which elicited general if critical appreciation from Cromwell, roused no interest in Henry who in vain glanced through that Aristotelian exercise for a foundation in Scripture.[31] Conventionally, Henry is supposed to have displayed a genuine and competent intellectual interest in theology, but even here some curious chinks appear. Stephen Vaughan, in 1531, decided not to send him certain Lutheran works, not (as might be supposed) because to do so might prove dangerous to himself, but because he knew the King would only give the books to others to read and advise him on their contents.[32] Cranmer, who knew Henry better than Vaughan, confirmed this when he told Capito that the King had followed his usual practice about a book sent to him; that is to say, unwilling to labour over it himself, he had given it to two people of opposite views to read and report on it, after which he would base his judgement on an assessment of their criticisms.[33]

How well this fits the general picture that is beginning to emerge – the picture of a nimble opportunist, picking up ideas and suggestions from all around him and putting together a usable amalgam – a kind of encyclopaedia article – without having to do the hard work himself. In scholarship as in policy, Henry, so to speak, used secondaries and did not go back to the sources. One may even wonder about his often stressed orthodoxy, allegedly founded on doctrinal learning of a professional kind. Certainly he was no Lutheran; but why did he leave his only son to be brought up by known reformers, and why did he appoint a regency council in his will which assured that Protestantism would triumph after his death? If he was really attached to the mass, to transubstantiation, priestly celibacy and the rest, he went a strange way about serving his faith when he called in Cheke to tutor Edward VI, imprisoned the Howards, and cold-shouldered Gardiner.

The King, therefore, was a man of great vigour, intelligence, shrewdness and skill, but also somewhat shallow and an opportunist whose only real programme concerned the advancement of his own interests by whatever means seemed suitable and possible in terms of both law and politics. Since opinion in his day largely identified the interests of king and people, his desires did not of necessity harm the realm, and his opportunism could easily advantage it. More often than not this happened, though at times Henry's essential lack of depth, his inability to think problems of government through, and his willingness to adjust to the pressures of the moment as long as the ultimate, always personal, end was kept in view, proved a drawback to those like More or Cromwell who saw more clearly and deeply. A total egoist is unlikely to be able to see anything clearly in the dazzle produced by his single guiding star. The King and the country were saved by the unexpected qualities which partly redeemed a really rather deplorable character. Henry knew how to take advice and delegate power, and he had perfect political instincts. Better men without these gifts have certainly done much greater harm; Henry VIII, neither a good nor a wise man, employed them to make himself into a great king. If he was not Pollard's great statesman on the throne, he was also far more than the bloated, lustful, capricious tyrant of popular mythology.

*   *   *

The historian has no easy task with Henry VIII. He must try

to escape from the sheer physical presence of this handsome giant with his bright and penetrating eye, his frequent joviality, his ready manipulation of men. On the other hand, he must not surrender to a natural revulsion against a man who constantly introduced personal emotion into politics, pursued vendettas, displayed brutal indifference or vindictive hatred where he had ceased to approve. Henry's qualities, good and bad, explain a great deal about his hold over the imagination of contemporaries and later generations alike. As a personal monarch he was superior to the petulant, self-willed and often incompetent Francis I, whose constitutional position was rather less hedged about by the laws and customs of his realm; he was rather inferior to the dedicated if unprepossessing Charles V. He ruled his realm, and his word was decisive in affairs. But it decided between and upon the ideas and the work of others. There is nothing very surprising in this, nor does it make him any less intelligent, quick-witted, or skilful. It means, however, that he lacked originality and far-sightedness, and probably also an understanding of fundamentals. Using the brains of other men, he added his own political dexterity and that immense strength of will which carried him through even when he could see no light in the darkness. In the hands of Henry VIII personal monarchy did not mean personal attention to the business of government, though it had done so in the hands of Henry VII. Nor did it mean the constant weighing up of conflicting counsel and the pursuit of a personal policy based upon a personal assessment, as it did for Elizabeth. It meant the putting of the King's personal force behind policies not of his devising. His greatness lay in the rapid and accurate interpretation of the immediate situation, in a dauntless will, and in his choice of advisers; but not in originality, and it is doubtful if he was the architect of anything, least of all of the English Reformation.

This is no denigration; it is an attempt to get things straight. A man of such evident power, equipped with such mixed qualities and presiding over such catastrophic events, raises a real challenge to any biographer, which perhaps explains why Pollard has been left for so long in occupation of the field. The next one, when he comes, may well end by agreeing with the final sigh of him who was the first to adventure upon that enterprise: 'To conclude: I wish I could leave him in his grave'.[34]

BIBLIOGRAPHICAL NOTE (1973)

Since this essay was written (1961), two important biographies of Henry VIII have appeared which once again interpret the king as the man in charge of his time, though they disagree about his psychology. J. J. Scarisbrick's magisterial *Henry VIII* (1968), which effectively replaces Pollard's as the king's standard biography, pictures an eclectic, capricious, unpredictable mind from which sprang both the ideas and the action which made up the politics of the reign. I have explained the reservations I have (despite my general admiration for the work) in the *Historical Journal*, vol. 12 (1969). Lacey Baldwin Smith's *Henry VIII: the Mask of Royalty* (1971) presents an essentially romantic portrait painted in purple, gold and black. His Henry VIII is both a perpetual adolescent and the sort of evil man who exercises a horrid fascination. I find some of the psychological insight highly convincing, but the details of the story as told by Mr Smith depend too often on some cavalier and approximate handling of the evidence. On reflection, it appears that both authors, convinced of Henry's political acumen and dominance, are yet driven to deny him consistency and foresight, or indeed the solider qualities which go to the making of the policies of power. Both, but especially Mr Smith, also think him highly complex where on another view he can appear straightforward enough. I would suggest that the difficulties which they set themselves to resolve and which in part defeat them arise from their determination to prove his primacy in affairs and his control. If one accepts, as even after these new studies I am still inclined to do, that Henry was rarely master of the (Europe-wide) events which affected him and that he needed other people to organize policy for him, his lack of constant purpose and the very variable success of the reign cease to be mysterious. At the same time, I concede that I have in the past underestimated his direct participation in government and his ability to turn acquired ideas into an intellectual system designed to support personal monarchy. I also think that, unable quite to forget Pollard, all of us with the exception of Dr Scarisbrick have underestimated the sheer mean horribleness of the man.

NOTES

1. J. A. Froude, *History of England*, vol. i, Preface.
2. Especially in *Henry VIII* (annotated edition, 1905) and *Factors in Modern History* (1907); but even a mature work like *Wolsey* (1929) still embodies a strikingly favourable view of Henry.

3. Especially F. Hackett, *Henry VIII* (1929). The author described himself as a 'psycho-historian'.

4. There are a few brief studies of which the best, beginning to see Henry VIII in a less Pollardian light, is that of Christopher Morris in *The Tudors* (1955). Prof. Bindoff's view in *Tudor England* (1950), esp. p. 96, tentatively modifies Pollard's but remains essentially based on it.

5. *Henry VIII*, p. 346. Of course, Pollard recognized Henry VIII's egotism (e.g. *Factors*, pp. 83 ff.), but he was throughout concerned to show that it did not matter.

6. For a prime recent example of the romantic view see L. Baldwin Smith, *A Tudor Tragedy* (1961), pp. 125 ff.

7. *Henry VIII*, pp. 363 f.

8. *Henry VIII*, pp. 409 f.

9. See my 'King or Minister? The Man behind the English Reformation', *History*, 1954, pp. 216 ff.

10. *Henry VIII*, pp. 56 ff.

11. *Letters and Papers . . . of Henry VIII*, xvi. 590.

12. Cf. my 'Thomas Cromwell's Decline and Fall', *Cambridge Historical Journal*, x. 150 ff.

13. Cf. D. B. Quinn, 'Henry VIII and Ireland, 1509–34', *Irish Historical Studies*, xii (1961), 318 ff.

14. *Letters and Papers*, xi. 501, xii. I. 1315.

15. *Henry VIII*, pp. 402 f.

16. G. R. Elton, *The Tudor Revolution in Government*, 1953, p. 281.

17. *Ibid.*, pp. 155 f.

18. G. R. Elton, *The Tudor Constitution*, 1960, pp. 126 f.

19. *Letters and Papers*, ix. 969.

20. E.g. *Letters and Papers*, iii. 165, 305, 357.

21. For this cf. the general argument of my *Tudor Revolution in Government*.

22. *Letters and Papers*, ii. 4512.

23. Cf. M. D. Knowles, 'The Matter of Wilton', *Bulletin of the Institute of Historical Research*, xxi. 92 ff.; G. R. Elton, 'The Quondam of Rievaulx,' *Star Chamber Stories*, 1958, pp. 147 ff.

24. *Letters and Papers*, ii. 2871.

25. *State Papers of Henry VIII*, i. 79.

26. G. R. Elton, 'Evolution of a Reformation Statute', *English Historical Review*, 1949, 174 ff.

27. Prof. R. B. Wernham in *English Historical Review*, 1956, p. 95.

28. See above n. 9.

29. Edward Hall, *Chronicle*, ed. 1809, pp. 864 ff.

30. Cf. Elton, *Tudor Constitution*, pp. 230, 357.

31. Cf. my 'Thomas Cromwell's Political Creed', *Transactions of the Royal Historical Society*, 1956, esp. p. 83.

32. *Letters and Papers*, v. 303.

33. *Ibid.* xii. II. 315.

34. Lord Herbert of Cherbury, *The Life and Reigne of King Henry the Eighth*, 1649.

PART THREE

Ket's Rebellion 1549

KET'S REBELLION 1549

by

S. T. BINDOFF

On 20 June 1549, the men of the town of Attleborough and of the neighbouring hamlets of Eccles and Wilby, in South Norfolk, threw down the fences recently erected by John Green, lord of the manor of Beckhall in Wilby, round part of the common over which they all had grazing rights. Their mission accomplished, they dispersed to their homes, and for over a fortnight there was no further trouble. But the weekend of 6–8 July found the men of these, and of many other, places congregated in the town of Wymondham to celebrate the festival of the Translation of St Thomas à Becket, whose chapel stood there. It was an opportunity for exchanging information about, and venting indignation at, local enclosing activities, as well as for hearing about the commotions already in progress to the south athwart the great road which linked Norwich through Wymondham, Thetford, Newmarket, and Cambridge with London. The upshot was that the saint underwent a novel translation, into a series of forays to throw down hedges on neighbouring manors. At this point a private feud intervened to become the starting-point of great events. Between John Flowerdew, a lawyer-turned-squire with an interest in two local manors, and the brothers Robert and William Ket, well-to-do tradesmen, there reigned a feud which owed its origin, or perhaps only its bitterness, to the discreditable circumstances in which Wymondham's great priory church had passed, after the Dissolution, into lay hands. It was Flowerdew's attempt, after his own closes had been thrown open, to bribe the rioters into doing the same to Robert Ket's, which brought together the two forces which were to make the Norfolk Rebellion – the

force of personality of a great leader of men, and the force
latent in the brawny arms and bucolic weapons of an angry
peasantry. We need not believe the high-flown words which
the chroniclers of the rebellion put into Ket's mouth on the
occasion, nor even that the scene was laid under the great oak
on the road between Wymondham and Hethersett which still
bears his name. It is enough for us that, on that 9 or 10 July
1549, the movement had found a leader.

*　　*　　*

It was with Ket at their head that the insurgents moved off,
on 10 July, along the road towards Norwich. As they went they
threw down more hedges and welcomed more recruits. At
Bowthorpe they were met by an ex-sheriff, Sir Edmond
Windham, who performed the Tudor equivalent of reading the
Riot Act by proclaiming them rebels and ordering them to
disperse. He only succeeded in annoying them and had some
difficulty in making his escape. As the company neared the city,
Ket demanded, but was refused, permission to march through
its streets to gain the spot, on its far, or north-eastern, side,
where he planned to establish his camp. He therefore by-passed
Norwich to the north, crossed the river Wensum at Hellesdon,
and on 12 July reached his chosen ground, the stretch of
common known as Mousehold Heath. Here he took possession
of Mount Surrey, the house which the sonneteer-earl had built
himself on the site of a dissolved priory, and made it his palace
and his prison. His followers, daily swollen by new arrivals
from far and wide, encamped on the high ground stretching
north and east from his headquarters.

For six weeks (12 July to 26 August) Ket maintained his
Great Camp on Mousehold Heath. Of the domestic organization of this vast *laager* something will be said later; here we
must confine ourselves to its external relations. The closest and
most continuous of these were with the City of Norwich. At the
outset the city authorities had shown themselves decidedly
hostile. But there was a 'fifth column' within Norwich, which

had used Ket's approach as a signal to lay open the Town Close, the ancient common, long since enclosed, on which grazed the freemen's cattle. These malcontents made common cause with the camp, and there was much going and coming between the two. In these circumstances discretion was certainly the better part of municipal wisdom, and during the first week several leading citizens, including the mayor, Thomas Cod, and a much respected 'elder statesman', Thomas Aldrich, were often in the camp assisting at its deliberations and urging moderation in its plans. These two even appended their signatures to the list of grievances which Ket and his governors drew up at this time. The Great Camp also stood close in relation with various other bodies of demonstrators abroad in the shire. The largest of these, drawn from the western hundreds, had assembled at Rising Chase, as Castle Rising was then known. Failing to seize Lynn, they moved south through Downham to the Suffolk border, where for some time they commanded the passage of the Little Ouse at Thetford and Brandon. Then they travelled east, to join Ket at Mousehold – bad strategy this, for had they 'dug in' at the river crossings they might have impeded the entry of government forces into the shire. Meanwhile, an attempt to seize Yarmouth also miscarried. A rising within the town, led by a group of men who had tried an unsuccessful *coup* there in the previous autumn, was reinforced from the Beccles-Bungay region of Suffolk. What exactly happened it is difficult to discover, but in the upshot the eastern insurgents, like the western, went to swell the thousands assembled on Mousehold.

There a new phase opened on 21 July with the arrival from London of York Herald with a promise of pardon to all who would lay down their arms and disperse. When Ket and the bulk of his following rejected this, saying that they had done nothing which called for pardon, the herald withdrew with the representatives of Norwich, and the city was hastily put into a state of defence. Cannonading began during the night and in the morning the insurgents swarmed to the attack. After some

fierce fighting they forced their way in through the Bishop's
Gate, and once inside quickly made themselves masters of the
city. The herald, after a further fruitless attempt to make an
impression, took his departure; the mayor and several aldermen
were carried prisoner to Mount Surrey; and for a time all
lawfully constituted authority came to an end. Later the mayor
was released and allowed to pass to and fro, while his deputy
restored some sort of order within the walls. The government's
answer to the seizure by popular insurrection of Norwich, the
second city in the kingdom, was the despatch of an expedi-
tionary force of about 1,400 men, among them some Italian
mercenaries, under William Parr, Marquess of Northampton,
brother to Henry VIII's last queen. Northampton entered
Norwich without opposition on 30 July. The next day his
troops beat off a determined attack from the camp, but on the
following morning a second attack led to a bloody contest on
Palace Plain, which so dispirited the marquess that he abandoned the city. The rebels then assumed complete control of
Norwich manning the gates, public offices, and prisons, and
installing themselves where they pleased, including the cathe-
dral. His success also encouraged Ket to make a fresh attempt
upon Yarmouth. He despatched 100 men, under three of his
Yarmouth supporters, to seize and hold the town for him. But
Yarmouth had taken fright at the goings-on in Norwich, and
instead of Ket's contingent the town admitted a naval squadron
under Sir Thomas Clere and Sir Thomas Woodhouse, two
local men, who took effective measures for its defence. The
attack which developed from the Lothingland side about the
middle of August achieved nothing but the destruction of the
harbour works then in progress, and cost the attackers six guns
and thirty men taken prisoner.

*   *   *

Meanwhile, in London the moral of Northampton's débâcle had
been learnt. During the second week in August, commissions
and instructions flowed out to all the shires around Norfolk for

the levying of troops. Letters went as far north as Doncaster, where Shrewsbury, President of the Council of the North, was ordered to have men in readiness to move. The Protector Somerset was originally to have taken command, but for reasons which we can only guess as he was replaced, on 9 August, by the Earl of Warwick. Warwick acted with speed and decision. He moved by Cambridge, Thetford, and Wymondham to Intwood, three miles from Norwich, where he arrived on 23 August. There he was joined by Lord Willoughby of Parham from Lincolnshire. He then disposed of 6,500 men, soon to be augmented by the 1,200 German mercenaries who were hurrying after him. From Intwood, Warwick sent a herald with an offer of pardon to all except Robert Ket himself. This was the third pardon offered, and it availed as little as its predecessors. On Saturday, 24 August, Warwick thrust his way into Norwich and after some street-fighting cleared it of rebels. But during the night some of them got in again and set fire to Conisford Street, which continued to burn all next day. This was Black Sunday for Norwich, with walls and gates broken, fire raging, troops everywhere, and outside the rebels continually on the prowl. Next morning, however, a dense cloud of smoke rising over Mousehold Heath showed that the rebels had fired their camp and were on the move towards Dussindale. There were more cogent reasons for their action than belief in the ambiguous prophecy that, as the current rhyme had it, Dussindale would be filled 'with slaughter'd bodies soon'; notably the fact that Warwick had cut some of their supply-lines and that to stay where they were would be to starve. But it gave Warwick the chance of using his cavalry, and on Tuesday, 27 August, he moved out with all his horse and 1,000 mercenary foot, leaving his English troops (who might not have stomached the task ahead) to guard the city. A final offer of pardon was made and refused, and then Warwick's professionals went to work. Ignoring the fact that the rebels had placed their gentlemen-prisoners in front as a screen, they charged and speedily broke up the undisciplined ranks opposing them. Then the cavalry got among the fleeing peasants and cut them down, to the number, it was said, of over three thousand. A late rally, which would only have cost more useless lives, resulted instead, if we are to believe one of the chroniclers, in the acceptance of the King's pardon read on the field at Warwick's orders.

Ket himself fled from the battlefield, but was soon caught and brought back to Norwich to await removal to London. A commission of oyer and terminer was sent down to deal with the horde of prisoners. How many were executed it is hard to say. A contemporary report speaks of 300, but reliable evidence relates only to the 150 or so who were hanged at Norwich. Not all were dealt with summarily, for in the following March twenty-nine men of Norfolk then in prison, and in the following May seventeen Suffolk men, were pardoned for their part in the rebellion, and individual pardons were issued for some time after that. Robert and William Ket were tried and condemned for treason in London on 26 November 1549, and were taken back for execution, Robert being hanged at Norwich Castle on 7 December and his brother from Wymondham steeple.

What we name, or misname, Ket's Rebellion began as a local riot, developed into a great popular demonstration, and ended in the violence and bloodshed of rebellion. These three phases of the movement, separated in point of time, also differ from one another in interest and emphasis. The first is an episode in the long-drawn-out conflict between landlords and tenants; the second turns on the relations between governors and governed, and its framework is the county; while in the third these local strands become interwoven with the thread of national politics.

*   *   *

The distinguishing thing about the events of the first phase, the phase of riot, is their lack of distinction. During the previous ten or fifteen years half a dozen, maybe a dozen, villages from one end of Norfolk to the other had been the scene of similar happenings. Two months before Attleborough's turn came, the Court of Star Chamber had been hearing evidence about a long-standing dispute, punctuated by violence, about common rights at Middleton; in 1544 there had been an enclosure riot at Great Dunham, in 1539 at Hingham. And what was happening in Norfolk was happening in almost every county of southern England. Everywhere landlords and tenants were at grips with one another, and the issues between them were variations upon a single theme, that complex theme which goes under the easy name of 'enclosure'. There would be little point in attempting to summarize, in half a page, the tangle of changes, and resistance to changes, whose unravelling occupies the four hundred pages of Tawney's *Agrarian Problem in the Sixteenth Century*. But it is both more feasible and more relevant to glance at some of the changes which had been taking place in the Norfolk countryside during the half-century preceding the rebellion. Under the early Tudors, Norfolk was already a name to conjure with in farming circles. The sandy loam of its north and east was most suited to barley, the boulder clay of its centre and south to wheat. The chalk ridges were also extensively tilled, but here the sheep was the indispensable adjunct of the plough, for the light soil was greedy of manure. On the marshlands of the west and of the north-west coast grazed large flocks of sheep. Only in the south-west, the Breckland, did Nature defy man's attempt to tame her; and where the Forestry Commission now wields its arboreal sway the rabbit was then the master. The county was thus well-placed to benefit from the growing demand for its two staple products, grain and wool. Norfolk corn-surpluses helped to feed London, as well as going north to Scotland and east to the Continent; Norfolk wool, besides supporting the native worsted industry, was in brisk demand both by the English and the foreign buyer.

* * *

The Norfolk peasantry, whose laborious alchemy transmuted

this rich earth into gold, was both a numerous and a prosperous race. The complicated tenurial arrangements obtaining in the county make it difficult to answer many of the questions which a statistically-minded age is disposed to ask. But we know enough to say that the proportion of freeholders who enjoyed a maximum of legal security with a minimum of tenurial obligation was higher in Norfolk and Suffolk than anywhere else in the country, being probably not less than one in three of the total. We also know that between the freeholders and the copyholders, those who held their land according to the custom of the manor, there was, instead of the fairly clear distinction which sometimes prevailed, the utmost confusion, with many individuals falling into both categories, a situation which promoted solidarity and with it security. The density of population meant that holdings were generally small – the average falling perhaps somewhere between five and ten acres – but a few acres of Norfolk earth were worth twice that number in a poorer county. Competition for land was exceedingly keen, and there was a brisk market for even the smallest portions; on some manors land was regularly bought on hire-purchase terms. It was in these countless small units that the business of producing Norfolk's grain was carried on. That business also yielded wool and meat in substantial quantities. Sheep were everywhere desirable, and on the lighter soils indispensable, fertilizing agents, and for them there awaited the shearer or the slaughter-house. And sheep and cattle depended, in their turn, upon pasture. A few peasants accumulated enough land to provide their own; but for the vast majority the only answer to the problem of where to graze their animals was the village common.

In marked contrast to the small-scale, predominantly arable farming of the peasants were the operations of their landlords. The landlords, or their lessees, had for the most part gone out of the corn-growing business and were devoting themselves to sheep and cattle farming. They were encouraged in this specialization by the existence of the institution, peculiar to East

Anglia, known as the foldcourse, or exclusive right of pasturing sheep upon specified areas, whether or not these belonged to the sheepmaster. Provided it were not abused, the foldcourse system could be mutually beneficial. But by making it possible for a man to rear large flocks without possessing land, it held the seeds of conflict between the two forms of land-utilization, and between the two classes which had become identified with them. A sheepmaster obliged to accommodate an ever-growing flock would be tempted to extend his grazing rights, if not by fair means, then by foul. Foldcourses might be converted into permanent sheepwalks by extinguishing the claims of others upon them; inconvenient enclaves could be absorbed, rights of way blocked, fences erected at strategic points. Above all, there were the commons, on which lords of manors usually enjoyed ill-defined rights of grazing sheep and cattle alongside those of their tenants. Most commons made far from ideal pasture, but on them a lord could dump his surplus animals, especially perhaps the inferior ones. Overstocking might be followed by enclosure, the lord appropriating a slice of the common contiguous to his land or foldcourse, on the plea that the tenants would be better off with what remained if it were relieved of his animals.

The resulting situation made exorbitant demands both on the land itself and on the patience of those whose livelihood depended upon its reasonable and moderate use. The ingenious theory which sees in the agrarian revolution of the sixteenth century the sole resource left to a countryside whose soil had been exhausted by the continuous cropping of the Middle Ages finds no support from East Anglia. But one can certainly imagine that if the oppression to which the soil of Norfolk was subjected in the early sixteenth century had been long continued the result might have been a Norfolk rebellion of another kind. However, it was the men who rebelled first. Between 1517, when Wolsey's commission investigated the progress of enclosure in the county, and 1549, the tale is one of perpetual disputes, riots, and lawsuits, some between rival landlords or rival villagers, but more between landlords and tenants. In 1520 it is Sir Henry Fermour who is accused of laying down sheepwalks near Fakenham, in 1539 Sir Henry Parker who is charged with encroaching upon Hingham Common; in 1540 it is Middleton Common, in 1544 Great Dunham, in 1548 Middleton again, which are in dispute. Fence-levelling had almost attained the status of a rural pastime by the time it reached Attleborough on that June day of 1549.

Agrarian grievances were to bulk large in the programme of the rebellion. Of its twenty-seven articles of complaint, thirteen relate directly to the situation outlined above. Several are self-explanatory: no lords to pasture animals upon the commons (this appears twice); copyhold land, meadow, and marsh all to be rented as they were in 1485; special rents payable by lords not to be passed on to tenants; land bought as freehold not to be converted into copyhold; no lord of a manor to be bailiff to any other; no man worth 40l. a year or more in land to keep sheep or cattle save for his own subsistence. A radical programme, indeed, which would have clipped the wings of rural capitalism. The inclusion of only one reference to enclosures, and that marred by an ambiguity which contrasts with the prevailing lucidity, is certainly a surprising feature; but it at least bears out the view, which is supported by other evidence, that in Norfolk enclosure as such was not the outstanding grievance that it was elsewhere. A demand for the enforcement of a standard bushel of eight gallons may reflect disputes arising out of the growing corn trade, while the restriction of the number of dovecots and the fencing-in of rabbit warrens were demands natural to a race of arable farmers who had suffered much from both.

*   *   *

The Attleborough riot had about it, as we have seen, a self-contained quality which gave no hint of what was to follow. It was at Wymondham, a fortnight later, that the local became general, the tip-and-run raid gave place to a major operation.

What took place there can be read in different terms; there was the time, the place, the man. Of the time we shall have occasion to speak later; it is enough to say here that there are grounds for regarding the few days about 8 July as of particular significance in the national pattern of events. The place, on the other hand, gives rise to certain reflections which call for discussion here. The strategic position of Wymondham needs no emphasis; any stimulus which the Norfolk movement received from outside the county it was most likely to receive by way of the great road on which lay both Attleborough and Wymondham. But Wymondham was more than a map-reference; it was a community, it was a meeting-place, it was still to some extent a place of pilgrimage. All these things may help to explain why Wymondham became the starting-point of the great demonstration. In particular, the fact that those who remained to scoff at their 'betters' had come, if not to pray, at least to attend a prayerful occasion, prompts the question whether there was any connection between the two forms of activity.

England in 1549 was in the midst of a religious revolution. Within the last generation Henry VIII had severed the nation's links with Rome and brought the Church of England under his sway. He had confiscated much of its wealth, he had executed some of its officers. But he had not tampered with its doctrine or ritual. The reformation of doctrine he had left, on his death in January 1547, to those who should govern in the name of his infant son. Within two years the Protector of the realm, the Duke of Somerset, and the Archbishop of Canterbury, Thomas Cranmer, had introduced a Book of Common Prayer which profoundly modified the historic doctrine of the English church. The compulsory adoption of this book on Whitsunday (9 June) 1549 was the first stage of the Edwardian Reformation. It was also the signal for a serious rebellion in Devon and Cornwall. The Western Rising, the first in point of time of the upheavals of that troubled year, was aimed almost exclusively against the government's religious policy. Largely officered by priests, the rebels demanded a return to the Henrician regime. For a few weeks they were dangerous. But they wasted time and energy over a fruitless siege of Exeter, and by the second week in August (that is, by the time that the government was taking serious measures against Ket) they had ceased to be more than the object of mopping-up operations.

Had religion anything to do with the events in Norfolk? Bearing in mind that the initial outbreak there took place within a fortnight of Whitsunday, that the movement proper began at a commemoration of the saint against whose cult Henry VIII had waged one of his bitterest campaigns, and that the feud between the Kets and the Flowerdews was bound up with the despoiling of Wymondham church, we should not be wholly surprised if the Norfolk rebels had proved as eager to defend the old faith against the new impiety as they were to defend its ancient monuments against their new despoilers. That, indeed, seems to have been the first interpretation placed upon their proceedings by Somerset and the Council. What, in their case, gave colour to the idea was the coincidence that the Princess Mary was residing at Kenninghall, barely two miles from Eccles, and that rumour had made her servants the instigators of the disturbances which broke out at the same time across the near-by Suffolk border.* For Mary was the heir-presumptive to the throne, and her religious views were, as the Council told her, 'such as are openly known to be against the proceedings of the King's Majesty and the whole realm, and such as (we fear) have given no small courage to many of these men to require and do as they do'. But Mary's answer, 'that all the rising about the parts where she was, was touching no part of religion', has also become the answer of history. Not only is it inconceivable that, if the men of Norfolk had shared Mary's abhorrence of the new dispensation, they would have ignored her presence as in fact they did, but the positive evidence about them all points the other way. The new Prayer

* Was it also coincidence that Eccles had a Catholic parson who was prosecuted in 1549 for saying Mass and Vespers?

Book which the Western Rebels likened to a 'Christmas-game'
was regularly used by Ket's followers for their open-air services
on Mousehold Heath; and it was to one of the 'new preachers'
that they turned for spiritual counsel. Nor, upon reflection, can
we imagine it otherwise. The county which had been a hot-bed
of Lollardry and Lutheranism, which was to have so high a
percentage of clerical ejections under the Marian Reaction, and
which in the fullness of time would become a stronghold of
Puritanism, was not the county to rise in defence of the Mass
or of the power of priestly order.

With religion in the sense of a particular set of theological
propositions the Norfolk rebels may have been unconcerned;
with religion in the sense of the proper discharge by its ministers
of pastoral duties they showed a quite lively concern. What part
the Norfolk clergy took in the rising is a question more easily
asked than answered. How exceptional, we may wonder, was
the vicar of North Elmham, who after it was all over had to
appear with other 'comrades' before the royal commissioners
at Fakenham, doubtless as an accomplice in his parish's remarkable piece of 'open conspiracy'? How typical the parson of
Gayton Thorp who was reported to have said that he wished
the town of Lynn and all the gentlemen in it were on fire?
On the whole, we may guess that the clergy in general held
aloof. There was certainly a good deal of anti-clericalism in the
insurgents' list of grievances: priests not to be allowed to
purchase any more land, and their present lands to be let to
laymen; those unable to preach to be dismissed and replaced
by others chosen by either parishioners or patrons; no priest
to be a gentleman's chaplain, but all to reside in their benefices;
all clergy with 10*l.* a year or more to teach poor children the
catechism and primer; tithes to be commuted at 8d. in the noble,
that is, at a flat rate of ten per cent. It is easier to believe that
the clergy stood outside rather than within a movement which
tabled such demands. The clergy could certainly not compete
in popular esteem with the churches. The parish churches of
East Anglia had long evoked a communal solicitude, and bene-

fited by a communal effort, probably unequalled in England. Even a priory church like Wymondham's owed much, including its remarkable west tower, to the parishioners who enjoyed only a part share in it. Few things were better calculated to add to the resentment generated by the agrarian troubles than the wave of spoliation which accompanied the dissolution of the monasteries and chantries and the outlawing of images, relics, and shrines. Men and women who had approved, or at least accepted, the desanctification of edifices and objects might none the less deplore the fate which overtook so many of them. Flowerdew's stripping of Wymondham has always found a place in the story of the rebellion. But may not Sir John Clere's looting of West Somerton, or the row over the sale of church property in Yarmouth, have made as many recruits for the cause?

And with religion in the sense of the moral basis of society? How far were Ket and his followers concerned with that? Their most famous demand reads as follows:

'We pray that all bond men may be made free, for God made all free with his precious blood shedding.'

This appeal to the Great Manumission of Calvary against the perpetuation of an obsolete social stigma may seem at first sight to reveal an urge towards the reconstruction of society upon Christian principles. And it is a fact worthy of remembrance that the only resounding denunciation of villeinage ever heard in Tudor England was uttered by the English peasantry in their hour of corporate articulacy. But we must beware of building too much upon these few trenchant words. It is possible that they were inherited, with one or two other ideas, from the Twelve Articles of the German Peasant Rising of 1525. Now in the German movement not only had serfdom been the leading issue, but the appeal to the New Testament, as expounded by Luther, had been the dominant note, so that this demand, in this form, had been the German peasants' veritable battle-cry. In the Norfolk of 1549 the situation was quite otherwise. There personal villeinage lingered on, it is true, perhaps more stubbornly than in any other part of England; and to those who bore its taint it was doubtless a life-long, indeed a more than life-long, slur. But their number was small, perhaps a few hundred, and the burden of their servility did not in practice weigh them down. Again, the very fame of Ket's demand for their emancipation rests largely upon its uniqueness in his catalogue. Here, and here only, does he base his appeal upon Christ and upon what was done in Judæa in the twentieth year of the Emperor Tiberius; elsewhere his appeal is to custom and to what was done in England in the first year of King Henry VII. It may be that Ket's own religious conviction was as deep as his moral sense was lofty, and that both found expression in his championship of the underdog of Tudor Norfolk. But this justly celebrated article affords no real ground for attributing to his movement a degree of religious fervour harnessed to a social egalitarianism which few, if any, of his followers can have shared.

After the time and the place, the man. Wymondham's greatest contribution to the rebellion was, of course, Robert Ket himself. Diligent research has failed to elicit much more than the three salient facts that Ket's forebears had been established in the district for several generations, that the family was closely associated with the church which Flower-dew looted, and that Robert Ket himself, by profession and property, must be placed somewhat above the middle of the social scale. All were excellent qualifications for the part which he was to play. But none can compare in historic importance with the personal qualities to which his leadership of the movement bears witness. It was because he possessed those qualities that Ket was offered the leadership; it is for the same reason that his acceptance was to mark a turning-point in the story. At that instant the movement underwent its first metamorphosis; the riot was over, the full-scale demonstration had begun. The cause may have produced the man; but it was for the man to make the cause.

* * *

The Norfolk movement surged forward where corresponding movements crumbled and broke because it was inherently strong and because it found a leader of first-class calibre. But is that the whole explanation? What took place in Norfolk in July 1549 was a monster breach of the peace, a complete, if temporary, breakdown of the machinery of law and order. The fact that nowhere else, save in Devon and Cornwall, was this breakdown so complete prompts the question whether there was not some defect in the machinery itself. It is a question which in the present state of knowledge may not be capable of answer. But one or two points suggest themselves. Sixty years of Tudor government had weakened, but not eradicated, the instinct by which each county looked for guidance to those who bore its chief dignities, lay and ecclesiastical. In the case of Norfolk these were the Duke of Norfolk and the Bishop of Norwich. The Bishop we can dismiss out of hand. William Rugge *alias* Reppes, who disgraced that office between 1536 and 1549, was a dead loss to both church and state. His dismissal would in itself almost have been worth a revolt, and one of the wholly commendable results of Warwick's punitive visit to Norwich was his enforced resignation. If Norwich was a broken reed, Norfolk was a bird in a cage. Thomas Howard II appears to have made himself no sweeter a name in local than in national history, and there is no reason to suppose that the rebels wasted emotion over the catastrophe which had befallen him and his son in 1546. They did not talk of their 'good duke' as the Londoners were to talk of Somerset when he joined Norfolk in the Tower. But good duke or bad duke, Thomas Howard had been a power in the affairs of his titular county, as well as in those of his country, for a generation before his fall. It was he who had built the palace at Kenninghall. He and his son also had three houses in Norwich and what was left of the medieval fortress of Castle Rising. When in 1525 East Anglia had staged its last major protest, against Wolsey's Amicable Loan, the Duke had been cast for the role of pacificator. His influence may have helped to restrain Norfolk from emulating Lincolnshire in 1536. In 1545 he had been made the first Lord Lieutenant of Norfolk and the neighbouring counties. Had he been available in 1549 he would have been the obvious man for the government to call upon. But before 1549 Howard was down. And his fall may have contributed something to the rebellion. For he had concentrated not only power and prestige, but also property, in the county. In particular he had received the lion's share, something like forty manors, of the monastic lands seized there at the Dissolution. Thus it was only after 1546 that the dispersal of these lands began in earnest. Of the Howard manors in Norfolk, twenty-two were settled in 1548 upon the Princess Mary, who thus came to reside at Kenninghall. But smaller parcels began to go elsewhere. Early in 1549, for instance, Richard Fulmerston, an ex-steward of the Duke's, bought all his property in Thetford, as well as some of his other Norfolk manors, one of which he sold (such was the momentum of the process) the day after he acquired it. At the same time the chantry lands, which by the act of Edward VI had followed the monastic lands into the hands of the Crown, began to follow them out again. The Norfolk chantries were surveyed early in 1548, and within twelve months many of them had been disposed of.

Is it fanciful to see in the fall of the great house a stimulus to the rivalries among the county families which had so long been constrained to pay it court and beg its favour? That fall created a vacuum in local politics which no other individual or family was sizeable enough to fill. But there were gentry enough and to spare ready to fight for the largest morsel of the wealth and power which now dropped, pancake-wise, among them. Norfolk had long been noted for the number of its gentlemen. Had not the Duke himself pointed to the fact in 1536 as a safeguard against rebellion? But the events of 1549 were to

belie him, and we are certainly disposed to see in their super-
abundance an element of weakness rather than of strength.
That it contributed to their unpopularity is undeniable; that it
helped to justify their unpopularity is likely enough. Intensity
of competition tends to vary with the number of competitors,
and the competition for wealth, place and prestige in the Norfolk
of 1549 must have been a fierce business. Such conditions do
not promote solidarity. Here and there we get hints of inter-
family feuds, Lestrange against Townshend and Knyvet, Drury
against Woodhouse, Paston against Clere. The Norfolk gentry
may have been caught in 1549 with its ranks divided.

One section of it flourished like the green bay tree, the
lawyers. The litigiousness of the county had long been pro-
verbial. In the previous century it had furnished the worst
spectacle of legal racketeering to be met with anywhere, and
the statutory limitation in 1455 of its attorneys to the number
of eight did not prevent it from continuing to have, in the
sixteenth, more lawyers than any other. The most enterprising
of them went to London to make their fortunes – the names
of Hobart, Yelverton, Gawdy and Coke are Norfolk names –
the stay-at-homes practised in Norwich, Yarmouth and Lynn.
The lawyer-turned-squire was the *bête noir* of the rebels of
1549. It was no accident that John Flowerdew, whose mis-
placed trust in the power of the purse helped to turn a riot into
a rebellion, was one of the tribe. Then there was Master Hobart
of Morley, son or grandson of Henry VII's attorney-general,
whose fences were levelled; John Corbet, a gentleman-lawyer
sprung from Norwich freeman stock, who in 1548 had bought
with another purchaser the chantry of Sprowston, and whose
house and dovecot there suffered at the rebels' hands; and
Thomas Gawdy of Harleston, who was taken prisoner. Their
dislike of lawyers also comes out in one or two of the rebels'
demands. Of particular interest is the request that no feodary
shall in future be legal adviser to any man during his term of
office. The work of the feodary, the county representative of
the Court of Wards responsible for all matters relating to land

held of the king by knight service, was peculiarly susceptible
to pressure by interested parties, and its severance from private
legal practice was a *sine qua non* of its honest discharge. The
demand that no one holding less than 10*l.* a year in land should
be required by the escheator or feodary to submit to an inquisition into his property was designed to protect the small
landowner from inordinate expense. But both demands gain
their chief interest from the fact that the escheator of Norfolk
during the year preceding the rebellion had been none other
than John Flowerdew of Hethersett. What tale of private
vexations, we may wonder, lies behind the bland impersonality
of these two demands?

The same circumstances which help to explain the origin of
the movement may also throw some light upon its development.
For the riots which heralded it no particular blame attaches
other than to the landlords who had invited them. Faced with
such local outbreaks, county officials could not be expected to
do more than to check their spread. But this is where the
Norfolk authorities conspicuously failed. It appears that the
demonstrators first incurred the censure of authority on 10 or
11 July, when the former sheriff harangued them at Bowthorpe.
By that time they were well on their way towards Mousehold
and were little disposed to abandon an enterprise so auspic-
iously begun. Windham's tone, moreover, was ill-suited to men
who did not admit that they were doing wrong. But might not
an earlier and more tactful intervention have checked the
movement, or better still have diverted it into a lawful channel?
The keen sense of order which, under Ket's leadership, per-
meated the whole undertaking would have favoured such an
outcome. But although we know that several justices of the
peace resided in the immediate neighbourhood, we hear of no
such attempt to intervene at this early stage. On the contrary,
the inactivity, tantamount to abdication, of the justices is, like
the silence of the watchdog in *Silver Blaze,* one of the most remarkable features of the story. The Norfolk commission of the
peace was a very full one, containing fifty-four names, forty-

six of them those of local knights and gentlemen. We hear very
little of these men during the rebellion, less still anything to
their credit. If it was public spirit which led Roger Woodhouse
of Kimberley to seek out the rebels at Hellesdon on 11 July,
bearing an olive branch in the shape of carts laden with bread
and beer, his ill-usage and captivity were certainly a poor reward. It was a pity that he was so unpopular. But the epic of
Nicholas Lestrange of Hunstanton, sheriff and knight of the
shire, makes sorry reading. He and Sir William Woodhouse
fled by cock boat into Lincolnshire, leaving his brother and son
as hostages, and Lestrange at least seems to have avoided going
back until he could tack himself on to Willoughby of Parham's
relieving force. Compared with this, Sir Edmund Knyvet's
sortie from his fortress of New Buckenham to attack a rebel
outpost sounds heroic. The silence which covers so many names
might, of course, have been an enforced one. But the reported
imprisonment of gentlemen in large numbers and from all parts
of the shire seems to be a legend. The gentlemen whom we can
prove to have been taken are very few, and all came from the immediate neighbourhood of the camp. Moreover, several of the
Norfolk J.P.s reappear in the train of either Northampton or
Warwick. The inference is that most of them 'disappeared'
during the storm, either lying low in their manor houses or,
like Lestrange, removing themselves out of harm's way.

They need not have been so scared. For a gentleman to fall
into the hands of the rebels was far less dangerous than for a
beaten rebel to fall into the hands of the gentlemen. There were
no hangings, no roastings in ovens, no torturings. Imprisonment
and baiting was the worst that would have befallen them until
the very end, when a place of danger on the battlefield became,
not without a certain grim justice, the final ordeal. But it needed
no other trial than the test of events to convict the knights and
gentlemen of Norfolk on the indictment against them – that
they were unfit to govern. They were unfit to govern because
they had proved themselves unable to govern; and they were
unable to govern because they had forfeited the respect upon

which government such as theirs rested. Immersed in their family fortunes, their fine houses (Norfolk is rich in early Tudor), their sheepfarms, their feuds and their lawsuits, they neither knew nor cared enough about what was going on around and underneath them. Sir Thomas More had described government in his day as 'a conspiracy of rich men seeking their own commodities'. The government of Norfolk in the years before the great rebellion must have approximated to that description.

*   *   *

We can dilate on the shortcomings of the Norfolk gentlemen because we know who they were. In attempting to appraise the deeds of the Norfolk rebels we are under the grave handicap of not knowing who they were. One of the overdue tasks relating to the rebellion is the compilation of a list of those who took part in it and of their places of origin; material is not wanting, and the result, however imperfect, could not fail to be instructive. Lacking such a list, we must do our best with the names available. A map showing the towns and villages represented by seventy of Ket's company reveals an interesting pattern. Over the greater part of the county the distribution appears fairly even, with a hint of two concentrations, one in the triangle Burnham-Lynn-East Dereham, the other along the axis Attleborough-Wymondham-Norwich. It is tempting to identify these two areas with the two main assemblages, at Castle Rising and Mousehold. The extension of the places involved into north-east Suffolk might similarly be linked with the attempt on Yarmouth. By contrast with this wide belt of country, stretching from the neighbourhood of Hunstanton on the Wash to that of Southwold on the coast of Suffolk, south-west Norfolk, that is, the region south and west of a line drawn from Lynn to Diss, is hardly represented at all. The omission of place names in this region from so fragmentary a list as ours would obviously be too slender a basis for theorizing but for two other facts. There is, first, the historical fact that of the eight Norfolk hundreds unrepresented in the only known list of Ket's governors, seven lie contiguously within this region and, indeed, taken together practically cover it. The inference is obvious, that Ket found least support in this part of the county. And this inference, in turn, tallies with the second fact, a fact of geography: the region in question includes what has always been the poorest and most thinly settled part of Norfolk. Here, it is safe to conclude, there was little of that pressure of wants upon land which prevailed elsewhere in the county; here, that is to say, there were largely lacking the conditions which gave rise to the rebellion. If we may accept this contrast between south-west Norfolk and the rest of the county in their attitude towards the rebellion, then its significance is readily apparent. It must have conduced to isolationism. Norfolk is bounded, as to roughly one-half, by the sea; and to rebels who were for the most part landsmen and who had in any case failed to seize a port, the sea was the limit of expansion. If, in addition, at least one-half of the remaining land-boundary constituted a sort of natural *cordon sanitaire*, then the rising must have been largely sealed off from the beginning. It is hard to believe that if Ket had staged a rising in, say, Warwickshire, it would have displayed the centripetal tendency which characterized the movement in Norfolk.

To say this, however, is not to make the mistake of representing this tendency of the Norfolk movement to look inwards rather than outwards as something imposed upon it by external circumstances instead of as something springing logically from its very nature. If Ket had wanted to emulate the Western Rebels by setting off for London, he could doubtless have done so. He might indeed have outdone them by reaching it, since he had less than half their distance to travel and no Exeter to mask or capture on the way. But such an operation formed no part of Ket's programme. To the Western Rebels the government of Westminster might be a hostile power to be persuaded or coerced into abandoning its religious policy; to the Norfolk rebels that government was an ally to be encouraged to persevere in, and to be helped to enforce, its agrarian policy.

It was the government on the spot which had to be supplanted, the man up at the Big House who needed a lesson. Ket remained in Norfolk because that was where his task lay. In leading his followers to Mousehold and making it the scene of a sort of vast sit-down strike Ket was obeying the inner logic of the whole enterprise. Here, on a site traditionally associated with popular movements – did they remember how their forefathers had gathered in 1381? – they would eat, drink, and be merry, worship God and live in brotherhood, debate and legislate and give good justice to their fellows. It was a grand concept, and the extent of its realization is a measure both of the spirit of the rank-and-file and of the genius of the leader. How easily might the whole thing have dissolved in dissension and ended in pantomime. But morale seems to have remained high and discipline good until the end, the bitter end. And, indeed, why should we expect it to have been otherwise? From the graveyard of Dussindale, from the charnel pits of Norwich, there sounds a ghostly challenge. What sort of people do they think we were? Do they think of us as a disorderly rabble consumed by greed, hatred, and lust to destroy? 'Not men but brute beasts indued with all cruelty', 'the refuse of the people' (for so our enemies called us)? For shame. We who lie here were honest, sober, sturdy folk, having God and the commonweal before our eyes. No hirelings we, but men with a stake in the country, having our farms and our flocks as our fathers had done before us. No simpletons, either, for whom law and government were bottomless mysteries. Was it not commonly said of us that we carried Littleton's 'Tenures' at the plough tail? And did we not, year in and year out, help to rule ourselves, in our manor courts and our courts leet, in our parish councils and on our sworn juries? How then should it be that, when we were met together for the redress of our just grievances, we should not quit ourselves like the law-abiding, order-loving, constitution-minded folk that we were?

No popular commotion was ever less like the conventional notion of a *jacquerie* than the Norfolk Rebellion, at least until a foretaste of its brutal suppression induced some lowering of its standards. Being arrived, with a minimum of disturbance *en route*, at Mousehold the company quickly constructed its own machine of government to replace the broken-down machine of the county commission. Under Ket himself as leader and supreme law-giver, there sprang into existence a 'county council' composed of two representatives of twenty-four out of the county's thirty-two hundreds, and of the city of Norwich, plus a representative of the Suffolk contingent. These representatives or governors, were doubtless men of standing in their own districts. One of the few of whom we know more than the name is Edmund Belys or Beles, who, with Robert Sendall, represented the hundred of Eynsford. Beles was a copyhold tenant of Lord Morley's at Twyford. Some twenty years before he had been stung into a protest, in the form of a Star Chamber bill, against the man who leased Morley's rights in the hundred and who was using the court leet as an engine of oppression. With such testimony as his to guide them, the rebels might well request the King to take back all leet jurisdiction into his own hands. Another governor (although here identification is not certain) was Thomas Clerke of Yarmouth. Clerke had been one of the accomplices in John Rotheram's attempt of the previous autumn to lay open the Yarmouth Town Close and in other ways to challenge the rule of the bailiffs. Despite his active part in the rebellion, he was one of those who survived its suppression (doubtless because he was then in the relative safety of Yarmouth gaol) and was eventually pardoned. William Doughty (North Erpingham) may have been the wickner or sub-reeve of the village of Southrepps; William Howlyng (Mitford) probably belonged to the well-to-do family of that name in Shipdam. Such stray identifications could doubtless be multiplied by methodical work among the local sources.

Of the rank-and-file we know even less than of their leaders. A list of forty-seven persons known to have taken part distribute themselves occupationally as follows: seventeen were husbandmen, seven butchers, four tailors, two labourers, two tanners, two fishermen, two millers, two coopers, two shoe-makers, with an inn-keeper, a mason, a baker, a water man, a hatter, a mercer, and a rat-catcher. Such a list, with its nursery-rhyme flavour, will at least serve to remind us that this was no exclusively agrarian movement. It had a considerable urban element, recruited principally from Norwich and Yarmouth, which were responsible for most of the trades enumerated above. But, to be sure, the antithesis which we make between town and country is far less valid when applied to their Tudor counterparts. Enclosure itself was not exclusively a rural phenomenon, witness the many town riots against it at this time. Conversely, the economic problems of town, like the depression of the worsted industry in Norwich, must have had repercussions in the surrounding countryside. In general, the evidence of the Norfolk rebellion bears out the view that the rising of 1549 was a rising of the common man, the man in the street as well as the man in the field.

*   *   *

The orderliness of Ket's demonstration was matched by the attention to form and procedure which characterized its public acts. What importance the demonstrators attached to this, and how they managed to achieve a standard answering to their wishes, appear from the story of Thomas Godsalve. Son of Sir John Godsalve, lawyer, clerk of the signet and comptroller of the mint, whose foxy features live for us in one of Holbein's most revealing portraits, Thomas Godsalve was one of the gentlemen carried prisoner to Mousehold at an early stage in the proceedings. 'At which time of his so being there' (so runs his own version of the episode) 'he was by the said Ket and divers other rebels then there assembled compelled as well to write such bills as were by the said rebels devised to be made and written as also to read such bills, complaints, writings and commissions as were brought or did come into the hands of the said rebels.' Godsalve, in short, acted as Ket's secretary of state.

His was the hand that penned those instruments, running in the King's name and issuing from 'the King's camp', by which Ket sought to govern Norfolk; his, too, perhaps, the hand which wrote the list of grievances for transmission to West-minster. For his misprision of treason, Godsalve afterwards pleaded the King's pardon and he was given office by Mary Tudor, whose godson he was. There was more in this obser-vance of forms than mere play-acting. Not only was it the way in which men like Ket and his governors, with their long acquaintance with affairs, might have been expected to act; it was the way in which, being launched upon their present enter-prise, they had to act. They sent out their writs in the King's name because they were about the King's business; they com-mandeered supplies after the manner of royal purveyors. Hav-ing supplanted the gentlemen who had so long misgoverned the county, they addressed themselves directly to their master the King in the manner of representatives asking for instructions and full powers. They wound up their list of grievances with the request that the King should commission their chosen leaders to purge the shire of evils and evil-doers.

How was it possible, we may ask, for a man like Ket to indulge in such a fantastic and fatal misconception? To rep-resent rebellion as an attempt to deliver a good king out of the control of evil counsellors was, of course, part of the stock-in-trade of the rebel in the age of personal monarchy. But Ket's appeal lay not to the King against wicked counsellors; it lay to the King's good counsellors against his wicked local officials. And the antithesis was no mere creation of a disordered mind. For in the summer of 1549 the King's counsellor-in-chief was the Duke of Somerset; and the Duke of Somerset was, in the eyes of the common man, the embodiment of that 'gentleness' which was so far to seek among the gentlemen. Had not Somerset, within a year of Henry VIII's burial, buried that monarch's ferocious treason legislation? Had he not re-estab-lished and revivified the Court of Requests, that Court of Poor Men's Causes in which the little litigant could find speedy

4—TT • •

and inexpensive justice? Had he not patronized that group, the 'commonwealth men', who were labouring to diagnose the causes of the country's economic ills and to prescribe remedies for them? Above all, had not Somerset addressed himself, the first leading statesman since Wolsey thirty years before, to the burning question of enclosure? His issue, in June 1548, of a commission to tour the counties chiefly affected by enclosure and to collect evidence on the spot was a gauge of his determination to make the statutes against enclosure something more than the pious futilities they had become. His poll-tax on sheep, in the following November, threatened to make the new sheepwalks not only illegal but – nightmare of nightmares – unprofitable.

This was royal counsel after the peasants' own heart. But they knew – who better? – the opposition which it would arouse and the scale of the effort needed to translate it into fact. What was their part to be? Official spokesmen urged them to do nothing except supply the commissioners with evidence of enclosures in their districts. It was unpalatable advice, but during the commission's first spell of work in the summer of 1548 the peasants seem to have done their best to abide by it. The result, to minds as angrily impatient as theirs, must have been disappointing. Only in a number of south midland counties had the commission really got to work; and there, while something had indeed been achieved, landlord obstructionism had already shown itself a formidable obstacle. By the spring of 1549 there must have been many who felt with Bishop Latimer that 'in the end of the matter there cometh nothing forth'. Somerset himself probably shared their feelings, for he returned headlong to the attack. In May 1549 he set forth another proclamation denouncing enclosures. On 14 June he issued a general pardon to those who had taken the law into their own hands by throwing enclosures open. This last date is significant: it was four days after the outbreak of the Western Rising, six days before the riot at Attleborough. Three weeks later came the real crisis. After a series of disturbances in all the surrounding counties, the men of south Norfolk assembled at Wymondham decided upon action. Simultaneously, government policy underwent its first significant change. Whether their coincidence in time sprang from any connection between these two events we shall probably never know. But if the leaders at Wymondham did receive any hint of what was happening in London, it might well have helped to make up their minds. For the news from London was of an onslaught upon Somerset's kid-gloved handling of riot and rebellion, an onslaught in which those who, like Paget, hated weak government were joined by those who, like Warwick, hated social reform. Shaken by the uproar in the country and by the accusations of his fellows, Somerset yielded, and during July a spate of instructions to local magnates and officials to repress disorder bespoke the change of attitude.

It was this change which converted the Norfolk demonstration into the Norfolk Rebellion. For it went far to destroy the two premises upon which, as we have seen, both the programme and the strategy of the movement were based, namely, that its aims were identical with the aims of the government, and that the government would welcome, or at least condone, what it was doing towards achieving them. The turning-point came with the arrival of the herald at Norwich on 21 July. In form, at least, the message which he delivered was conciliatory. The King's offer to fix the rents payable next Michaelmas at the level which had obtained forty years previously, and to hold down the price of wool, was accompanied by an invitation to the assembled commons to depute four or six of their number to draw up a list of grievances: Parliament, the King added, would be summoned at the beginning of October to pass the necessary legislation. Thus far, both in content and tone, the pronouncement echoed the 'gentleness' which had marked Somerset's earlier words and deeds. But it was accompanied by two riders which struck a different note: one was the demand that the multitude should disperse forthwith, the other an offer of pardon to all who should do so. If the offer was unwelcome because of its implication that the men of Norfolk had transgressed in staging their massive 'participation', the demand was unacceptable for its intention to dissipate the only force capable of achieving their aims, the force of numbers. Let the Great Camp appoint its prolocutors, let these set forth their proposals, but once the mighty host had melted away who would be there to see that they too did not dissolve into nothingness? The best that could be looked for – and that only so long as Somerset retained some influence and the Western Rebellion continued to impose prudence – was that the Great Camp should commit suicide, the worst – and it would soon come to this – that those who refused this way out should be crushed as a salutary warning to others. That was the brutal truth of the matter; but it was a truth which men who had set out in the opposite belief found hard to swallow. The effect may be gauged from what followed. The withdrawal of those – the few, we may imagine – who chose to accompany the herald only purged the camp of its weaklings, and on the next day Ket committed his one act of unprovoked aggression, the attack on Norwich. How far, granted the essential rightness of his cause, he was justified in this is a moot point. He may have argued that, since he could not maintain his camp next to a hostile city, it was better to seize Norwich before the townsmen could arm against him. But the deed itself, and its consequences, certainly gave colour to the view that he and his followers were too dangerous to be spared.

*   *   *

The government's next emissary was Northampton, with his puny force. Perhaps there were no more troops to spare, and the government had to make the familiar choice between sending too few or too late; perhaps Somerset cherished the illusion that to send an inadequate force was to avoid bloodshed. But Northampton's failure, and Russell's victory in the west, left no room for further argument. It only remained to settle who should have the credit, or bear the opprobrium, of taking command. Somerset's original appointment, and subsequent replacement by Warwick, have in retrospect a symbolic quality; but we do not know why either took place. Somerset might have reduced the slaughter; but apart from that it mattered little to the peasants by whom they were cut down. Their cause was already lost. They had only to go down fighting.

BIBLIOGRAPHICAL NOTE

The reappearance of this essay, which was written as a *pièce d'occasion* on the quartercentenary and was reprinted a few years ago, can be excused only on the ground that it has yet to be superseded by a full-scale study. Such a study, in the form of a thesis for a higher degree of the University of London, is, however, now nearing completion. Its author, Mrs Marjorie Power, has kindly drawn my attention to several errors of fact in my original text and these I have corrected: but I have made no attempt to amend its more substantial shortcomings (for example, in the fragmentary analysis of the rebels' occupations) in the light of her superior knowledge.

All accounts of Ket's Rebellion have been largely based upon one, or both, of the two near-contemporary narratives, Nicholas Sotherton's 'The Commoyson in Norfolk, 1549' (British Museum, Harleian MSS., 1576, 564 ff.), and Alexander Neville's *De furoribus Norfolciensium Ketto duce* (1575; English translation by Richard Woods, 1615). Sotherton, member of a well-known Norwich family and brother to the Leonard Sotherton who played a minor part in the events of 1549, furnishes a well-informed eye-witness account; Neville's version owes its value to his intimacy with Archbishop Parker, who as a young man had addressed the assembly at Mousehold. The only other near-contemporary versions which have any independent value are those contained in Holinshed's *Chronicles* (1578) and Hayward's *Life and Raigne of King Edward the Sixt* (1630). Of the half-dozen rehashes of this material to appear within the first three centuries of the events themselves the most careful and complete was that given by Blomefield in his *Essay towards a Topographical History of Norfolk* (ed. 1805–10, iii. 220 ff.). The appearance in 1859 of Rev. F. W. Russell's *Kett's Rebellion in Norfolk* was a landmark in the historiography of the subject. Russell supplemented the literary sources by a wide range of record material, while his grasp of the nature of the movement enabled him to do it far greater justice than his predecessors. After Russell the first two important contributors were A. F. Pollard, who in his *England under Protector Somerset* (1900) and in the opening chapters of his *History of England from the accession of Edward VI to the death of Elizabeth* (1913) elucidated the political setting of the upheaval of 1549, and R. H. Tawney, whose *Agrarian Problem in the Sixteenth Century* (1912) set it firmly in its context of rural change. One of Professor Tawney's pupils, Mr R. J. Hammond, examined the background of the Norfolk movement in detail in his unpublished London M.A. thesis, 'The Social and Economic Circumstances of Ket's Rebellion', to which I acknowledge my own indebtedness. By contrast, J. Clayton's *Robert Kett and the Norfolk rising* (1912) adds nothing to either knowledge or understanding of the subject.

Within the last few years Pollard and Tawney have in their turn been revised and amplified in two authoritative works, Professor W. K. Jordan's *Edward VI: The Young King* (1968) and volume IV of *The Agrarian History of England and Wales*, edited by Dr Joan Thirsk (1967). Mr A. Fletcher's *Tudor Rebellions* (1968) provides a comparative study, and the local scene has been illuminated by Dr K. J. Allison's articles on Norfolk husbandry (*Agric. Hist. Rev.* V, 12–30 and *Econ. Hist. Rev.* 2nd ser. XI, 98–112) and Mr J. F. Pound's analysis of Norwich society (*Past and Present* no. 34, 49–69).

PART FOUR

Tudor Enclosures

TUDOR ENCLOSURES*

by

JOAN THIRSK

Glossary

In the first two decades of the century, Tudor enclosures received more than their share of attention from economic historians. Since then there has been no attempt to reconsider the old judgements in the light of new knowledge, and by constantly rehearsing old views we are now in danger of over-simplfying a complex problem.† In the crudest accounts the movement is described thus: all over England men were enclosing their land and turning it into sheep pasture, because the wool of the sheep was more profitable to grow than any other produce on the farm. Enclosures were carried out with ruthless disregard for the rights and interests of the smaller farmers and cottagers, and were the cause of much misery and social unrest.

A moment's reflection must raise doubts concerning the accuracy of this account, for, apart from the fact that not all land is suitable for sheep, we learned more than thirty years

---

* *To enclose:* To fence or hedge or otherwise enclose a piece of ground which has hitherto lain open, either in the arable fields, or the meadows, or on the common pastures, and thereby to restrict, or more usually, to extinguish altogether common rights of grazing thereon.

To engross: To amalgamate two or more farms for occupation by one farmer. Such consolidation involved leaving one farmhouse empty, or reducing its status to that of a cottage, since it was deprived of most of its land.

Stints: Village regulations dictating the number of cattle, sheep, and horses which a manorial tenant with common rights might put in the open fields and meadows after harvest and on the common pastures.

† See the bibliography at the end of this section.

ago from the study of the London food market in the sixteenth century that there was much specialization in food production in the different regions of England.[1] The Londoner's mutton came from Gloucestershire and Northamptonshire, his fruit and hops from Kent, his vegetables from Essex, his dairy produce from East Anglia, his bread corn from Sussex, Kent and Norfolk, the barley for his beer from Lincolnshire. This picture of agricultural diversity and regional specialization, which is equally familiar in present-day Britain, does not accord well with the England described in the enclosure story. The truth is that enclosures took many different forms. They were carried out for many different reasons. They frequently resulted in a change of land use but not always in a change from corn-growing to sheep-keeping. In short, they varied greatly in character and importance from one part of England to another.

Types of Enclosure in the Sixteenth Century

Briefly, one may define enclosure as a method of increasing the productivity or profitability* of land. This definition would apply accurately to all forms of enclosure. To appreciate both its social and economic significance in the sixteenth century, however, it is necessary to bear in mind that not all parts of England at that time were at the same stage in agrarian development. The process by which the open field system gave

* By 'increase in the productivity of land' I do not mean to suggest that the yield of crops per acre necessarily increased. It may have done but this is difficult to prove. I mean simply that the land was more efficiently cultivated. Pasture closes were grazed more carefully than commons. Arable closes were better manured and might carry a crop in the fallow year. In the words of the author in the *Discourse of the Commonweal of this Realm of England* – 'Experience sheweth that tenauntes in common be not so good husbandes as when every man hath his part in several.' Also experience showed that land was not always being put to its best use. Old arable fields were not as productive as ploughed-up grassland. See the reasons for the proposed enclosure of the lands of Mudford in Somerset in 1554 in *Tudor Economic Documents*, ed. Tawney & Power, I, pp. 61–2.

way to consolidated farms in separate ownership was long and
slow in some areas, and relatively rapid and painless in others.
In the southern and eastern counties of Essex, Surrey, Sussex,
and Suffolk and in the south-western counties of Devon and
Cornwall examples of common field farming were hard to find
in 1500. The densely settled parts of the midlands were then
at a far more advanced stage of enclosure than the thinly
populated counties of the north. Finally, there were yet other
districts where it is believed that common fields had never
existed, though it is probable that such areas lay always in
thinly-populated pasture-farming regions where the arable fields
were small in size.[2]

Over a large part of central and northern England, there was
still much commonable waste and common field in the sixteenth
century. Indeed, much survived into the eighteenth and nineteenth centuries. And because enclosure was a long drawn-out
affair in many places, some regular stages in the process of
evolution through the centuries can be discerned. In the first
days of settlement it can be assumed that most villages had
small arable fields and meadows, while the remainder of the
village lands – the pasture and the waste – was extensive. Indeed, the waste of one village was not clearly marked off from
the next, so abundant was it on all sides that a strict definition
of boundaries between townships was for a long time unnecess-
ary. Intercommoning by the stock of neighbouring villages or
parishes continued for centuries in many places, since it saved
the expense of constructing a boundary bank between them. As
population increased, the arable fields had to be enlarged at the
expense of the pasture and waste until a point was reached
where the common grazings failed to feed all the stock of the
inhabitants. Intercommoning between parishes often caused
disputes and litigation at this point, and commons were formally
carved up between townships. The next step was to control the
number of stock which individuals might graze on the commons. Part of, and later all, the common waste was turned

into regulated common pasture where animals were stinted, and feeding was restricted by agreement to certain periods of the year when other grazings, the stubble of the open fields, for example, and the aftermath of the meadows, were not available. Further increases in the human and animal population of the township might later compel fresh reductions in the stints previously agreed upon. Finally, when land shortage again became critical and all these measures of economy had been tried, the final expedient was the enclosure and division of both common pastures and common fields among individuals. It might be carried out on individual initiative with the lord's consent or without, and it might raise an outcry or pass unnoticed. Alternatively, it might be carried through by communal agreement, a method which became more common in the later years of the sixteenth century, and was fairly usual in the seventeenth. In either case enclosure meant that all common rights over the fields or commons were extinguished. When enclosure of the fields took place by agreement, it was often accompanied by a re-arrangement of strips so that some consolidation of holdings could be effected. When common pastures were enclosed, parcels were allotted to all who claimed common rights, including both cottagers and peasants holding strips in the open fields. In all cases, each man was master of his own piece of land, to hedge or fence it, and cultivate it as he pleased.

It may be that no single English village passed through all the stages described here in converting its arable fields and commons into consolidated farms. But in the sixteenth century every one of these stages in development could be illustrated by examples from different regions of England. The partitioning of commons between several parishes was a frequent occurrence in the Pennine areas in the Tudor period. Henfield Common in the Lancashire parish of Whalley, for example, was divided between the townships of Clayton-le-Moors, Altham and Accrington between 1576 and 1594. Thealmoor, near Oldham, was divided between the lords of Chadderton,

Alkrington, and Nuthurst prior to 1526.[3] The enclosure of
part of the waste in order to create some regulated common
pasture, where the quality of the grazing could be improved
and better shelter provided for stock, was undertaken in James
I's reign on Bowes Moor in Yorkshire and in Charles I's reign
at Wath-upon-Dearne, near Rotherham.[4] In Elizabeth's reign,
energetic colonization of the waste in order to increase the
ploughland was carried out at Burton Leonard in the West
Riding, where the number of holdings was increased from
sixty to eighty-four oxgangs. The inevitable sequel was a pasture shortage which compelled the inhabitants to reduce the
stint of cattle allowed to every oxgang from seven beasts to
four.[5] The introduction of cattle stints on formerly unstinted
common pastures was discussed in parts of the Lincolnshire
fenland at the end of the sixteenth century, though nothing
came of the proposal.[6] A reduction in the old cattle stints owing
to the increase in the number of stock was forced on the
villagers of Burton Leonard, Bishop Wilton on the Yorkshire
wolds, and Foston in the western clay vale of Lincolnshire.[7]
Finally, the division of the common fields and pastures among
individuals was under way in countless villages all over the
country. In some cases, it was carried out by agreement, as at
the enclosure of Bradford Moor in Yorkshire in 1589 when all
the tenants assembled on the moor and reached an almost
unanimous decision to enclose. In others it was a matter of
individual initiative. On many Lancashire manors in Rossen-
dale piecemeal enclosure of an acre or two of waste, or the
enclosure of a few strips in the arable fields, was extremely
common. These closes were made by tenants with the lord's
consent and most of them aroused little or no opposition. In
other cases, eager landlords were prepared to buy consent, as
did William Brocas of Theddingworth in Leicestershire, who
in 1582 granted 'diverse gratuities and leases of good value' to
secure his tenants' cooperation. The enclosures which caused
indignation and the breaking down of hedges were those in

which a lord or his tenant rode roughshod over the rights of others. These were the cases which enraged public opinion and lingered long in popular memory. They also supplied the fuel that inflamed the writings of contemporary pamphleteers. Nevertheless a determined tenantry, jealous of its rights and willing to raise a 'common purse' to pay the costs of litigation, got many such wrongs righted. A victory of this kind seems to lie behind the decree of 1569–70 ordering Thomas Saville of Woodkirk to lay open an enclosure of a hundred acres which he had made on the commons of Allerton township in the parish of Bradford. The decree was awarded 'after complaint by the tenants and freeholders thereof'.[8] The many other enclosure cases heard in the courts of Westminster combine to portray a far from docile peasantry, invoking 'ancient custom' to good effect. They did not all submit and depart from their villages with tears and lamentation.

Since enclosure of one kind or another was in progress over the greater part of England in the Tudor period, all attempts at generalization about the movement are hazardous. Nevertheless it is certain that some kinds of enclosure were more typical of some regions than of others. The partition of waste between intercommoning parishes, the construction of regulated common pastures on formerly unregulated waste, the taking in of waste on a large scale in order to increase the arable land – these forms of enclosure were most frequent in the more thinly settled parts of highland England – in the Pennine districts of the north, for example, from which most of the cases quoted above are taken. Land there was extensively rather than intensively cultivated. There were still abundant wastes awaiting improvement to accommodate any increase of population. If, for the greater convenience of working, enclosure of the arable fields took place in such areas, it was frequently done by amicable agreement or by piecemeal enclosure initiated by individuals and it raised no great opposition. The inhabitants were not yet oppressed by a threatening land shortage, and did not consider their interests seriously injured. This fact, indeed, affords a clue to the way in which enclosure probably took place in the Middle Ages before population pressure and the existence of a growing class of poor landless villagers underlined the distressing social consequences of enclosure more heavily than the economic advantages.

In parishes of moderate population density where the problem of grazing shortage was new in the sixteenth century, or in pastoral regions like the fen where the population was large but where, owing to the nature of the economy, the common pastures were still extensive, the introduction of stints on the commons, or the reduction of old ones, was a frequent expedient for sharing the land more equitably. It served as a warning signal of land shortage ahead, but did not betoken any immediate crisis. There are many examples of new stints being introduced in the townships of the midlands and in the vale lands of northern England in the sixteenth century, for these were areas which had attracted early settlement, and were populous and relatively intensively cultivated. Finally, there were many townships in the same region which experienced an even more serious land shortage, where the waste was already taken up, the common pastures were inadequate, and where enclosure, in consequence, invariably injured someone. In such villages enclosure of any kind was liable to lead to violent protest.

Motives for Enclosure

This attempt to differentiate the character of enclosure in the various regions of England assumes that at each stage the ultimate stimulus was a rising population, compelling individuals or whole communities to devise more economical ways of using their land. It was a powerful underlying motive, particularly in the midlands, but it was not the only one. In the sheep-rearing uplands, where settlement was often thin, and the sheep-walks and hill-grazings extensive, rising prices seem to have exerted more influence than pressure of population. Indeed, to many contemporary writers, the inflation of food-prices, which made farming more profitable and gave the incentive to in-crease production, seemed a more powerful factor than land shortage, though the two were, of course, closely connected. Then, too, every landlord and every farmer had his own private reasons. Some landlords wanted to increase the value of their land in order to raise rents.* The lord of Honington in Lincoln-shire, Sir Charles Hussey, confessed himself obliged to enclose land in order to increase his income and meet the cost of ex-pensive lawsuits. Some large farmers decided to enclose and convert their land to pasture in order to reduce their labour costs, for, in the words of a contemporary, 'nothing is more unprofitable than a farm in tillage in the hands of servants where the master's eye is not daily upon them'.[9]

All the subsidiary motives for enclosure have to be con-sidered when evaluating regional differences of pace and pur-pose. But only the overwhelming compulsion of population increase, together with accompanying price rises, can explain why enclosure made such swift progress and was such a burn-ing issue in two separate periods of history, the sixteenth and the late eighteenth and early nineteenth centuries. Contem-poraries were more acutely aware of the relationship between population and land use than later historians. As the inhabi-tants of Bradford in Yorkshire explained when defending their decision to enclose the common, the population of the town had increased and the ancient land in cultivation was no longer sufficient to maintain them. When the inhabitants of four

* See, for example, the enclosure history of Cotesbach in Leicestershire. This is also an excellent example of a village wholly enclosed in the Tudor period, partly by force, partly by the buying out of freeholders, where much of the land was converted to pasture, but not apparently for sheep. Depopulation occurred, but it was the result rather of engrossing and rationalization of an estate. L. A. Parker, 'The Agrarian Revolution at Cotesbach, 1501–1612', *Trans. Leics. Archaeolog. Soc.*, XXIV, 1948, pp. 41 ff.

Lancashire townships fell out over the sharing of their commons, one of the causes of acrimony was the fact that forty new tenements had been built on the demesnes of Sawley Abbey since the Dissolution, thus aggravating the pasture shortage. People who had once taken a lenient view of intruders claiming common rights became more watchful as their waste land diminished while the scale of farming and stock-keeping increased. A native of Holme-on-Spalding Moor put the point succinctly when giving evidence in an enclosure dispute heard in the Court of Exchequer in 1620. He knew not whether a tenement built on the common some sixty years before had common by right or 'by sufferance or negligence of the freeholders'. But at the time the cottage was built 'the freeholders made little reckoning of common for so small goods as was then put upon the said common by the said tenants'.[10]

Government Enquiries and Legislation

Since enclosures in the sixteenth century were diverse in type and purpose, it follows that not all enclosing farmers were bent upon converting their ploughland to pasture. That the Crown was interested only in enclosure accompanied by conversion was due to the fact that such a change of land use led to unemployment and depopulation, reduced the corn harvest, and aggravated local problems of grain scarcity. At the same time, contemporaries were well aware that enclosure was not the only cause of these troubles. Engrossing was equally important, for, when two or more farms were thrown together, the superfluous farmhouses were either reduced to the status of cottages or left to decay. Thus the number of holdings in a township was reduced, the smaller farmers were deprived of a livelihood, land hunger and unemployment ensued. The result was a further increase in social tension.

When the first enclosure commission was appointed in 1517, its enquiries concerned enclosure and imparking and embraced the whole of England except the four northern counties. The Crown was not sufficiently well-informed at that time to recognize nice regional differences in the geographical pattern of enclosure, nor to appreciate subtle differences between enclosing and engrossing.* The commission appointed in 1548 was directed to enquire into engrossing as well as enclosing and imparking, but it did not complete its work, and the only returns which have survived relate to Warwickshire and Cambridgeshire. Even more short-lived was the commission of 1565, the only known returns of which relate to Buckinghamshire and Leicestershire. Nevertheless, it may not be without significance that these fragmentary reports relate to counties in central and eastern England. For in 1607, following upon the Midland Revolt, the enclosure commissioners finally centred their attention upon this area. Their articles of enquiry included both engrossing and enclosing, and their work was limited to seven counties, Warwickshire, Leicestershire, Lincolnshire, Northamptonshire, Buckinghamshire, Bedfordshire, and Huntingdonshire, counties which had lain at the centre of the disturbances and where, it was now recognized, the problems of enclosure and engrossing were most acute.[11]

The agrarian statutes and proclamations of the period likewise reflect a growing understanding of local differences and changing economic conditions governing the motives for enclosure. The first general statute of Henry VII's reign against the pulling down of towns (1489) aimed at arresting all depopulation and all conversion of arable to pasture irrespective of region and motive.† Later statutes, however, attempted to differentiate. In 1536 the Act of 1489 against depopulation and the conversion of ploughland to pasture was re-enacted, but it now applied only to the Isle of Wight and a group of counties in central England, extending from Lincolnshire and Nottinghamshire south to Berkshire,

* For the discussion by modern historians whether engrossing also meant enclosing, see below, pp. 114-5.
† There was one earlier local act concerning the Isle of Wight (1488) against enclosure and engrossing.

Buckinghamshire, and Hertfordshire, east to Cambridge and west to Worcestershire, and including Leicestershire, Rutland, Warwickshire, Northamptonshire, Bedfordshire and Oxfordshire. A second statute of 1533 attacked engrossing by prohibiting farmers from occupying more than two farms unless they lived in the parishes in which they were situated, and forbidding them to keep more than two thousand four hundred sheep. The preamble of the Act expressly described engrossing as a consequence of 'the great profit that cometh of sheep'. But in 1555, the conversion of arable to pasture was not ascribed to this one cause, but to the profits of cattle and sheep fattening which tempted men to specialize in this branch of farming at the expense of rearing. An Act of that year obliged farmers who kept more than 120 shear sheep to keep at least two milch cows and rear one calf. In 1593 the abundance and cheapness of corn caused Elizabethan legislators at last to shed their fear of enclosure and pasture farming and to repeal their acts to maintain tillage, but this opened the flood-gates to fresh enclosures, and, following the bad harvest of 1595, panic caused them to be revived. Again it was the graziers as well as the sheepmasters who bore the brunt of government opprobrium. It was enacted that land that had been under the plough for twelve years continuously before conversion to pasture should be restored to tillage. Nevertheless, an exception was made of land which had been grassed down in order to regain heart. Moreover, the Act applied in certain counties only – in twenty-three English counties, and in the Isle of Wight and Pembrokeshire. It excluded from its scope much of East Anglia, the south-east and the south-west, as well as Staffordshire, Shropshire, Cheshire, and Lancashire.*

In summary, therefore, it may be said that enclosure and the conversion of arable to pasture featured prominently in legislation throughout the Tudor period, but many of the statutes and proclamations were selective in their application and they give no grounds for asserting that enclosures were considered

* The act was later amended to exclude Northumberland also.

to be the responsibility of the sheepmaster alone, nor that sheep were deemed the sole cause of depopulation. Engrossing as a cause of depopulation was deplored in the proclamations of 1514 and 1528, the Act of 1533, the proclamation of 1548, the enclosure commission of the same year, the proclamation of 1551, and the enclosure commission of 1607. Indeed, it is difficult to explain why historians in recent years have so often seemed to forget that engrossing *and* enclosure were regarded by contemporaries as twin evils in the countryside and *equally* injurious to the commonweal. It may be that Professor Gay won a silent victory when, at the turn of this century, he engaged in long argument with I. S. Leadam whether the engrossing of farms necessarily meant that such farms were also enclosed.[12] Gay held that it did, and evidently persuaded others besides himself. More recent work on regional diversity, however, suggests that Gay was wrong in making this dogmatic, universal assumption. To take but one contrary example, the Lincolnshire marshland was a region little troubled by enclosure and conversion in the Tudor period. Nevertheless, it was much concerned with engrossing in 1607. The demand for fattening land was keen, not only from local farmers but from others living on the neighbouring wolds who reared on the hills and fed in the lowlands. In consequence, when farms were thrown together, or marsh pasture near the coast was leased to 'foreigners' living at a distance, houses of husbandry were deprived of their land and left to fall into decay. Here was a region plagued by engrossers and depopulation, but not by enclosers. Indeed, much of the land in the marsh was not enclosed until after 1800.[13]

Enclosure and the Pamphleteers

Like the legislation, the pamphlet literature of the time dealt with a variety of agrarian grievances and did not confine itself to enclosures for sheep pasture. Sir Thomas More's devastating

attack on the sheep which devoured men, and on the covetous
gentry who enclosed and depopulated without remorse for the
sufferings of the poor, lives longest in the memory. But more
than one pamphleteer and preacher reserved his strongest
language for engrossers of farms.[14] Others wrote not of sheepmasters alone, but of graziers, using the more general term to
embrace men who specialized in cattle rearing, fattening, and
dairying. Yet others deplored the sheep, not because sheep
inevitably followed enclosure (as they doubtless knew, there
were many farmers who overgrazed the commons with larger
and larger flocks without enclosing any land), but because sheep
drove out cattle and corn.[15]

Enclosure Disturbances

When agrarian discontent flared into open revolt in 1549, the
riots likewise disclosed a tangle of motives and more than one
cause of complaint. Ket's followers in Norfolk in 1549 did not
feel themselves so much injured by enclosure as by the over-
grazing of the commons by greedy lords, the damage done to
crops by the keeping of dovecotes and by rabbits kept in
unprotected cony warrens, as well as by rising rents. The only
reference in Ket's programme to enclosure is ambiguous and
appears to relate to closes for the growing of saffron.[16] The
Midland Revolt of 1607, however, was directly concerned with
enclosure and the conversion of ploughland to pasture. And
since the rebellion was concentrated in this one part of England,
in Warwickshire, Leicestershire, Northamptonshire, and
Bedfordshire, we shall illuminate the problem of enclosure by
considering why this was so.

Enclosure in the Midlands

In the first place, the midland counties, generally speaking, were the most densely populated in common-field England by 1500.[17] In Leicestershire there was no waste left except in Charnwood Forest. All the land not under the plough nor reserved for hay consisted of regulated common pasture.[18] The situation was probably little less serious in neighbouring midland counties. But while an increasing population in already congested townships was liable to precipitate some enclosure, since a change of this kind permitted the more economical use of land, not all densely-settled villages underwent an enclosure crisis in the sixteenth century. Much depended on the type of economy prevailing in the region, the nature of the soil, and the number of freeholders involved. In 1607, for example, the enclosure commissioners reported over 13,000 acres enclosed and converted to pasture in Lincolnshire. Yet almost nothing came to light in the fenland.[19] The reason lay in the pastoral nature of the economy. The fenlands, which lay under water in winter, afforded rich and abundant common grazing in summer. The native peasant got his livelihood from fattening stock on these pastures and required only a little land under crops to supply his household needs and to fodder his beasts in the hardest months of winter. In addition, he had other sources of income in the fish, fowl, and reeds of the fen. He had no need to convert old cornland to grass for he enjoyed unstinted common grazing. If he enclosed at all he was more likely to enclose grassland to increase his corn acreage.[20] In the marshland areas along the Lincolnshire coast, a system of mixed husbandry obtained. The arable usually occupied a larger proportion of the land of a township than in the fen and the grazings were less extensive (in most marshland villages stock were stinted on the common), but this was a recognized sheep and cattle fattening region, and probably had been for centuries. A satisfactory balance between arable and pasture had been struck long ago and charges of enclosing and converting arable to pasture puzzled the inhabitants. Their lands were 'such as time out of mind have been used for feeding and breeding or grazing of cattle and be not fit for tillage'. The local people were much more concerned in 1607 with the engrossing of farms by ambitious yeomen and gentry.[21]

Generalizing from these examples, we may infer that the market conditions of the sixteenth century were not of a kind to alter significantly the pattern of land use in old-established cattle fattening regions. It is probable that meat and wool yielded a satisfactory profit throughout the century. A fair balance between corn and grassland had been struck long before, which it was convenient to maintain. And the fact that most pastures, in the fen at least, were open commons was not yet regarded as a grave drawback to the majority. This, as we have seen, was due partly to the type of husbandry, but it must be attributed also in part to the class structure of fen society. The villages were composed of many small freeholders who drew more benefit from the use of open commons than they would have done from a small allotment of enclosed grassland. The situation might have been different had the fenland been populated by a smaller community of large farmers who could each have claimed large allotments after enclosure.

If the traditional cattle fattening regions of England were not troubled by enclosure and conversion, in what farming regions did they present a grave social problem? Until a comprehensive study of husbandry and enclosure in the sixteenth century is completed, the answer to this question can only be put forward tentatively. But it would seem that the problem was concentrated firstly in the densely-settled claylands where a mixed farming was generally practised, and where crop rotations that included some years of leys suited the land best and enabled farmers to keep more stock, when market conditions favoured them. The problem was concentrated secondly in the more thinly-populated chalk and limestone uplands where rearing was already the rule and where sheep were now being kept on a larger scale than ever before. In these two farming regions there were substantial differences in the circumstances surrounding enclosure.

The claylands were mostly populous areas of ancient settlement and relatively intense cultivation, where the need to use the land more economically was a powerful stimulus to the would-be encloser. Farmers were coming to recognize that flexibility of land use on the clays was a wise measure for increasing productivity. Some of the clays were so ill-drained as to make bad cornland and promised a greater yield if put down to permanent pasture, others yielded better under a convertible husbandry of alternate crops and leys. Under the common field system farmers had already been able to put this knowledge and experience to good effect by laying down land in the arable fields under temporary grass. Sometimes whole furlongs were left in ley by communal agreement, sometimes individual strips. In the latter case the farmer had to hurdle or tether his animals while they were grazing during the corn-growing season. When the harvest was carried, his strips were thrown open together with the stubble of his neighbours' lands to be depastured by the stock of the whole village. The only drawback to this practice, in some places at least, was that so many beasts had to be tethered that there was constant danger that they would break loose and trample down the corn. The peasants of Fulbeck in Lincolnshire explained that they had to tether three hundred head of draught cattle and milch cows and in 1620 decided it would be easier to enclose their fields.[22] This was the conclusion of many another farmer, though not everyone was able to procure the assent of his fellows.

It is evident from the answers given by farmers in star chamber to the charge of enclosing and converting arable to pasture that many changes of land use in the midlands which were reported to the enclosure commissioners in 1607 sprang from the decision to adopt some form of ley farming in enclosures – to rest the overworked ploughland and increase fertility by introducing a few years of leys. The advantages were expounded by Fitzherbert in these words: 'If any of his three closes that he had for his corn be worn or wear bare, then he may break and plough up his close that he had for his leys, or the close that he had for his common pasture, or both, and sow them with corn, and let the other lie for a time, and so shall he have always rest ground, the which will bear much corn with little dung.'[23] His opinion was not that of an unpractical crank. It was current among many thoughtful, observant farmers, and, indeed, its wisdom was finally recognized in Tudor statutes against enclosure. The Act of 1597 explicitly allowed the temporary conversion of arable to pasture in order to regain heart,* thus following the advice of the Speaker of the House of Commons, who had ventured to put a more moderate view of enclosure now that popular antagonism had somewhat abated and had condemned the old laws against enclosure for 'tyeing the land once tilled to a perpetual bondage and servitude of being ever tilled'.[24]

There is no need to press the evidence further and to take the more extreme view, once put forward by Miss Harriet Bradley, that the purpose of alternate husbandry was to rest the old arable because it was utterly exhausted by centuries of cultivation. The modern proponents of ley farming have never suggested that it is a desperate remedy for exhausted cornland. It has been recommended rather as a means of increasing the yield of both arable and pasture, since, by taking the plough all round the farm, the pasture benefits from being cropped (it is much easier to produce a good pasture that will last three or four years than to keep permanent grass in peak condition) while the arable is greatly improved by a period of rest under grass.

By adopting a more intensive system of husbandry on the claylands, farmers were able to keep more cattle and horses, and, if the land was suitable, more sheep – in other words, to produce more of the things that commanded a high price in the sixteenth century. But to place the emphasis on sheep at the expense of cattle is to falsify the picture of the economy of the claylands. Beef and leather were as much a product of the vales of England as mutton and wool. Whether prices favoured the production of cattle rather than sheep, or sheep rather than cattle, is another question which historians have not yet

* See above, pp. 113–4.

seriously tackled. Indeed, it is doubtful whether any generalizations could ever be made on this subject – so much depended
on the type of farm and the place of stock in the management
of the land. In the same way, it is impossible to make any
accurate statements concerning the relative profit from corn-
growing and stock-raising at this time. It is probable, however,
judging by contemporary opinion, that throughout the sixteenth
century animal products gave a larger margin of profit to clay-
land farmers than crops.* Hence the popular hostility towards
encloser and grazier. Not every enterprising farmer was both,
but the two were naturally identified in popular complaint.

The second farming region which suffered most from
enclosure in the Tudor period was the sheep rearing lands, the
less fertile uplands where from time immemorial sheep had
ruled the earth. They grazed the hillsides during the day and
were folded on the low fields at night. Indeed, without the
golden hoof, the land could not have been kept in cultivation.
In considering why enclosers gained such a strong foothold
here, it is necessary to remember that the uplands were areas
of large farms and small and sparsely distributed settlement.
The large farmer wanting to enlarge his sheep flock found it
easier to enclose great tracks of common or to force the
enclosure of the open fields, because his tenants were few and
the opposition weak. It is no accident that so many deserted
villages are found in the uplands, on the chalk wolds and on the
limestone and Cotswold hills of the midlands. It would have

* According to Fitzherbert, writing in 1539, 'of all stock the rearing of
sheep is most profitable'. While this may well have been true in the 1530s,
subsequent legislation (see above p. 114) suggests that it did not remain
true in the later decades of the century. Dr Bowden has suggested that the
price relationship between wool and wheat changed in the course of the
century, causing sheep pastures to expand at the expense of cornland in
the first half of the period and to shrink in the second. This conclusion
concerning price movements may well be correct but the suggested consequence, namely an increase in arable at the expense of pasture in the
later years of the century, is still disputed. It is equally likely that falling
wool prices were offset by good prices for mutton. Cf. P. J. Bowden,
'Movements in Wool Prices, 1490–1610', *Yorks. Bulletin of Economic
and Social Research*, IV, 1952.

been difficult, indeed impossible, for a landlord, however ruthless, to depopulate a large village.[25]

The economic incentive to enclose land in the uplands was the same as that which goaded the lowland farmer – the high price of animal products, particularly wool and mutton. In the first three decades of the century the booming textile industry created an almost insatiable demand for wool. It is probable that the market slackened off in the middle of the century as wool production increased and the broadcloth industry became depressed. But it is unlikely that the upland farmer's income was much affected by this. He now had to meet a growing demand for mutton for the townsman's table.* In addition, his sheepwalks produced a fine short wool which became more scarce and sought after as the century wore on. Larger sheep flocks in the vales, marshes and fens had increased the proportion of long coarse wool to such an extent that the fine wool of the hill sheep was at a premium.[26] The sheep flock had always been indispensable to the hill farmer, but in the Tudor period it did more than fertilize his fields; it paid his rent, furnished his house, and fed and clothed his family as well.

If we seek an example of a county where much enclosure took place but where several different motives were present, it is ready to hand in Leicestershire. It was not one of the main corn-exporting counties since it lacked good transport facilities to London and the coast.[27] Its speciality was cattle and sheep. In west Leicestershire, in the neighbourhood of Charnwood Forest, enclosure strengthened the hand of farmers specializing in dairying and rearing, some of whose land was converted after enclosure to permanent pasture, some adapted to a convertible husbandry.[28] In south Leicestershire, fattening was the main pursuit. Indeed, the permanent pastures of the Market Harborough district have continued to hold their fine reputation to

---

* One pamphleteer, writing in mid-century, implied that the popular taste for mutton was growing at the expense of beef. 'The most substance of our feeding was wont to be on beef, and now it is on mutton. And so many mouths goeth to mutton which causeth mutton to be dear.' *Tudor Economic Documents*, III, p. 52.

this day. In the eastern uplands, the sheep flock was the farmers' best friend and the price of wool and mutton the chief spur to his enterprise. In this way the whole of Leicestershire was exposed to the currents of agrarian improvement. No doubt a similarly varied pattern would emerge from a more detailed examination of the movement in other midland counties.

Conclusion

When Edwin Gay examined the enclosure evidence collected by the commissions of enquiry in the Tudor and early Stuart period, he suggested that the complaints against depopulating enclosure were somewhat exaggerated. If one measures the importance of the problem from a national standpoint, this may be a fair judgement. Also it was doubtless true, as John Hales declared in Edward VI's reign, that the worst and most ruthless enclosures had already occurred before the beginning of the reign of Henry VII. But this was cold comfort to the husbandman of the sixteenth century watching the progress of enclosure in and around his own village. Enclosure has first to be recognized as a social problem concentrated in the midlands. Seen in that narrower context, it cannot be lightly dismissed. In Leicestershire alone, more than one in three of its 370 villages and hamlets underwent some enclosure between 1485 and 1607.[29] The motives and incentives to enclose, as we have seen, were many and complex. But they worked their worst effects in one consolidated belt of country, stretching from the western half of Lincolnshire through Northamptonshire and Leicestershire to Warwickshire and reaching south to include Bedfordshire and Buckinghamshire. The historian who tries to account for trends and changes in a broad context recognizes different types of enclosure and different motives and thereby deepens his understanding of the causes of change. He sees the problem of the sixteenth century as a temporary crisis only. But the midland

peasant lived in the midst of events and saw only one widespread movement to enclose and convert the land to pasture.
He saw more cattle and more sheep in the closes. He saw rich
farmers taking up more and more land but giving less employ-
ment than ever before to the labourer. He could have viewed
the matter calmly had he lived in the Lincolnshire fens or the
Yorkshire dales. He could have viewed the matter in better
perspective had he lived to see the amiable enclosure agree-
ments of the seventeenth century. But it was difficult to keep
a balanced outlook when one's own livelihood was at stake,
and when, moreover, the idea of enclosure had not yet
'hardened and become more durable'.*

BIBLIOGRAPHICAL NOTE

The first attempt to examine the contemporary literature and explain the
causes of sixteenth-century enclosure was made by Erwin Nasse in a
paper *On the Agricultural Community of the Middle Ages and Inclosures
of the Sixteenth Century in England* (original edition, 1869; English
translation, 1870). Since this essay argued that the purpose of sixteenth-
century enclosure was to facilitate ley farming, it deserves more attention
than it has received in the present century. Nasse's conclusions were
accepted by W. Cunningham in *The Growth of English Industry and
Commerce* (1st edn. 1882), and with some modifications by W. Ashley in
An Introduction to English Economic History and Theory (1st edn. 1893).
They were afterwards neglected, however, perhaps because a more extreme
interpretation of the evidence of ley farming was put forward by Harriet
Bradley in *The Enclosures in England – an Economic Reconstruction*
(1918). Her argument that enclosure was due to soil exhaustion was challenged and discredited by Reginald Lennard in 'The Alleged Exhaustion
of the Soil in Medieval England', *Economic Journal*, no. 135, 1922.

The discussion took on a more statistical character when the reports
of the enclosure commissions of 1517 and 1607 were analysed. See I. S.
Leadam, 'The Inquisition of 1517', *Trans. R.H.S.*, 2nd Ser., VI (1892);
VII (1893); VIII (1894); XIV (1900); *The Domesday of Inclosures,
1517–18* (1897); E. F. Gay, 'The Inquisitions of Depopulation in 1517
and the "Domesday of Inclosures"', *Trans. R.H.S.*, 2nd Ser., XIV,
1900; 'Inclosures in England in the Sixteenth Century', *Quarterly Journal
of Economics*, XVII, 1903; 'The Midland Revolt and the Inquisitions of

* Polydore Vergil in 1534, quoted by M. W. Beresford, *op. cit.*, p. 104.
These words are adapted from Vergil's remark on the abuses of fifteenth-
century enclosure. I do not think that the idea of enclosure became generally acceptable until the mid-seventeenth century, when the last anti-
enclosure bill was presented in the House of Commons and rejected.

Depopulation of 1607', *Trans. R.H.S.*, 2nd Ser., XVIII, 1904. The use of these returns was severely criticized in E. Kerridge, 'The Returns of the Inquisitions of Depopulation', *English Historical Review*, 70, 1955.

Many of the contemporary pamphlets and sermons referring to enclosure may be found in volumes published by the *Early English Text Society* and the *Parker Society* respectively. A full list is included in Conyers Read, *Bibliography of British History, Tudor Period, 1485–1603* 2nd ed. (1959), pp. 218 ff.

Other work bearing on general problems of enclosure is contained in M. W. Beresford, *The Lost Villages of England* (1954), and P. J. Bowden, 'Movements in Wool Prices, 1490–1610', *Yorks. Bulletin of Economic and Social Research*, IV, 1952. This article was criticized in two subsequent issues of the *Bulletin*, and a reply published in vol. IX, no. 2, 1957. The most recent accounts of enclosure history are contained in *The Agrarian History of England and Wales, vol. IV, 1500–1640*, ed. Joan Thirsk, 1967, chs. I, IV; and M. W. Beresford, 'Habitation versus Improvement: the Debate on Enclosure by Agreement', in *Essays in the Economic and Social History of Tudor and Stuart England in honour of R. H. Tawney*, ed. F. J. Fisher, 1961. For a full and up-to-date bibliography of the subject, see J. G. Brewer, *Enclosures and the Open Fields: a Bibliography* (British Agricultural History Society, 1972).

NOTES

1. F. J. Fisher, 'The Development of the London Food Market, 1540–1640', *Econ. Hist. Rev.*, V, 1934–5, pp. 46–64.

2. H. L. Gray's map of open field England in *English Field Systems* (1915) has been provided incorrect. The map printed by C. S. and C. S. L. Orwin in *The Open Fields* (1938), p. 65, is much more detailed and accurate, though it too requires some minor revision. There are no counties in England in which some traces of common field cultivation have not been found. See also Joan Thirsk, 'The Common Fields', *Past and Present*, no. 29, 1964 and the ensuing debate in nos. 32 and 33, 1965, 1966.

3. Lancs. County Record Office, DD. Pt., Bdle 18; H. T. Crofton, 'Moston and White Moss', *Trans. Lancs. & Cheshire Antiq. Soc.*, XXV, p. 51.

4. P.R.O., *Exchequer Depositions*, 17 Jas. I, Hil. 1; Sheffield Central Library, WWM, C2, 257 (3).

5. P.R.O., *Exchequer Depositions*, 38 Eliz., Easter 1.

6. Joan Thirsk, *English Peasant Farming*, p. 112.

7. P.R.O., *Exchequer Depositions*, 38 Eliz., Easter 1; 14 Jas. I, Mich. 8; Thirsk, *op. cit.*, p. 97.

8. P.R.O., *Duchy of Lancaster*, 44, 440; *Victoria County History of Leicestershire*, II, p. 203; G. H. Tupling, *The Economic History of Rosendale*, Chetham Soc., LXXXVI, *passim*; Leeds Public Library, *Stansfield Collection*, C, 4, 1, 797. For an example of a common purse collected by tenants to pay the costs of an enclosure suit, see the case brought by the tenants of Holme-on-Spalding Moor against enclosers of their common – P.R.O., *Exchequer Depositions*, 19 Jas. I, Trin. 5. For

other examples, see R. H. Tawney, *Agrarian Problem in the Sixteenth Century*, p. 330, note 2.

9. P.R.O., *Star Chamber*, 8, 17, 24; Sheffield Central Library, *Strafford Letters*, WWM, 20a, no. 17.

10. *Duchy of Lancaster*, 44, 440; *Exchequer Special Commissions*, 2747; *Exchequer Depositions*, 18 Jas. I, Hil. 15.

11. The commissioners appointed in 1517 were ordered to report on the villages and houses pulled down since 1488, the land then in tillage and now in pasture, and the parkland which had been enclosed for wild animals. For the exact terms, see *The Domesday of Inclosures, 1517–1518*, ed. I. S. Leadam, I, pp. 81–3. For those of 1548, see *Tudor Economic Documents*, I, pp. 39–41. For those of 1607, see L. A. Parker, 'The Depopulation Returns for Leicestershire in 1607', *Trans. Leics. Archaeolog. Soc.*, XXIII, 1947, pp. 14–15.

12. E. F. Gay, 'Inquisitions of Depopulation in 1517 and the Domesday of Inclosures', *Trans. R.H.S.*, N.S., XIV, 1900, pp. 240 ff.

13. Joan Thirsk, *op. cit.*, pp. 238, 148–51, 154–6. On the question of engrossing and enclosing, see also the similar conclusions from different evidence of Maurice Beresford in *The Lost Villages of England*, pp. 113–5.

14. See the sermons of Hugh Latimer, Thomas Lever and Archbishop Cranmer, and William Harrison's *Description of England*, ed. F. J. Furnivall, 1876, p. 19 ff.

15. See, for example, the writings of Alexander Nowell and also *Certain Causes gathered together wherein is shewed the decay of England only by the great multitude of sheep*, reprinted in *Tudor Economic Documents*, III, pp. 51 ff.

16. Agrarian grievances may have helped to foment trouble in 1536 but enclosure complaints were not openly expressed in the Pilgrimage of Grace. Professor Bindoff in his re-examination of Ket's rebellion has pointed out other special local circumstances to explain why the outbreak in 1549 was centred in Norwich and its neighbourhood. Ket drew his support not from the thinly settled and poor soils of the breckland in south-west Norfolk but from the populous north and east where farms were already small, freeholders numerous and pressure on the land was becoming acute; cf. S. Bindoff, *Ket's Rebellion, 1549* (above, pp. 77–81, 92–3).

17. Cf. H. C. Darby, *The Historical Geography of England before A.D. 1800*, p. 232.

18. Cf. W. G. Hoskins, 'The Leicestershire Farmer in the Seventeenth Century', *Agricultural History*, xxv, p. 10.

19. J. D. Gould, 'The Inquisition of Depopulation of 1607 in Lincolnshire', *Eng. Hist. Rev.*, July 1952, p. 395. Land enclosed and converted to pasture amounted to 5,500 acres in Lindsey, 3,360 acres in Kesteven, and 560 acres in Holland, the fenny division of the county.

20. These points are elaborated in Joan Thirsk, *op. cit.*, p. 6 ff.

21. *Op. cit.*, pp. 154 ff. The quotation may be found in the answer of Francis Megson of Orby when charged with enclosure in Star Chamber in 1608 – P.R.O., *Star Chamber*, 8, 17, 23.

22. P.R.O., *Chancery Proceedings*, C. 2, Jas. I, F.13, 5. In Wigston Magna (Leics.) in the seventeenth century one-fifth of the open fields were in leys, cf. W. G. Hoskins, *The Midland Peasant*, p. 23.

23. *Tudor Economic Documents*, III, p. 23.

24. Cited in Harriet Bradley, *The Enclosures in England – an Economic Reconstruction*, 1918, p. 99.

25. Maurice Beresford, *The Lost Villages of England*, pp. 247 ff.

26. P. J. Bowden, 'Wool Supply and the Woollen Industry', *Econ. Hist. Rev.*, Second Series, IX, no. 1, pp. 44 ff. Dr Bowden's argument must be modified in the light of genetic considerations. See *Agric. Hist. Rev.*, XIII, 2, 1965, pp. 125–6.

27. John Gould, 'Mr Beresford and the Lost Villages', *Agric. Hist. Review*, III, 1955, p. 112.

28. *Calendar of State Papers Domestic, 1629–31*, p. 490.

29 L. A. Parker, 'The Agrarian Revolution at Cotesbach, 1501–1612', *Trans. Leic. Arch. Soc.*, XXIV, p. 41, note 2.

PART FIVE

John Knox

JOHN KNOX

by

J. D. MACKIE

During his own lifetime John Knox was engaged in violent disputes, and throughout the succeeding ages his character has been the subject of acrimonious controversy. To some of his contemporaries he appeared as the apostle of eternal truth divinely inspired, to others as an architect of evil. Later ages saw him variously as a stirrer-up of strife, the founder of the Protestant kirk, the perverter of reform into devious ways, the father of intolerance, the hero of the everlasting verity, the destroyer of the old and the beautiful. For centuries he was, despite all criticism, one of the heroes of Scotland. Latterly there has been an attempt to show him as the man who robbed Scotland of her heritage of art and enjoyment and plunged her into the ugly gloom of a perpetual Sabbath wherein the Calvinistic elect found their main pleasure in denouncing the shortcomings of blinded ritualists. And now the wheel comes round full circle. The latest biographers have seen a human Knox, a victim of his own intensity, hardened into bitterness by cruel experience, but spending himself ungrudgingly and fearlessly for a cause which, as he was sure, was destined to succeed in the end because it was the very cause of God Himself. One thing must be noted, that while there is an infinite variety of opinion as to his character, there is complete unanimity as to his importance. Love him or hate him, revere him or deride him, this was a man. For good or for ill he set his stamp upon the Scottish nation. It is absurd to describe him as the 'maker of the Scottish Reformation', which was made by no one man and which was begun before he took a share in it; but to that great movement his indomitable energy and his unquestioning faith gave a purpose and direction which marked it for all time.

The Scottish Reformation was part of a world movement which affected the whole of Christendom at the close of the Middle Ages; it was part of that rebellion of the facts against the theories which is called the Renaissance. In Scotland, as elsewhere, the 'Reformation' was produced partly by political and economic causes; there, as elsewhere, the condition of the Roman church invited criticism, and there, as elsewhere, new ideas had come in. In Scotland the old church had become the ally of economic privilege and the ally of France against England, and there the dissatisfaction with the existing religion had been heightened by an infusion of Lollardy from England, Lutheranism from Germany by way of the Low Countries, and a more resolute theology from Switzerland. This was introduced, probably in 1543, by George Wishart, who translated into Scots the first *Helvetic Confession* wherein it is clearly stated that the subject's duty to obey the 'magistrate' is limited by the obligation of the magistrate to use his power for the promotion of godliness. Whilst Wishart was active in Scotland some of the 'Anglophile' lords proposed to Henry VIII a plan for the murder or kidnapping of Beaton, and their intermediary was 'a Scottish man called Wyssher'. It is possible that in these hard times the missioner was also the plotter, though this is far from certain. Wishart was arrested in the house of a Lothian 'Anglophile' in December 1545, and on 1 March 1546 he was burned as a heretic (not hanged as a traitor) in St Andrews. On 29 May, Beaton was murdered by a small party of Wishart's admirers who had seized the castle of St Andrews and who held it until the balance of power was altered by the death of Henry VIII in England and the accession of the martial Henry II in France. The castle surrendered on 30 July 1547; the garrison was taken to France and some of the prisoners were sent to the galleys. Among these was John Knox.

The Early Life of John Knox

It is as a follower of Wishart that Knox makes his first appearance upon the historic stage. He was present at Haddington in the winter of 1545 bearing 'a twa-handed sweard, which commonly was caryed with the said Maister George'.

Who, then, was this Knox? Our knowledge of him is at once very intimate and very limited. As Raleigh said of Shakespeare, 'he wove upon the roaring loom of time the garment that we see him by'; it is from Knox's own works that we learn most about the writer, and for his biographer his works are a tantalizing authority. His minor writings, theological and exhortatory, show us his spirit and occasionally shed light upon his ordinary life. His letters tell us much, but they must be handled with some care; for Knox, though his actual conduct of politics was fumbling, added to the fire of the visionary a surprising political wisdom, and his correspondence may not always express his whole mind. It is in his *History of the Reformation in Scotland* that the essential Knox reveals himself most plainly as the leading actor in a great event; but even there Knox the autobiographer is secondary to Knox the historian.

For Knox, history recorded the unending struggle between God and the devil, and in that struggle he had been called to play a part; when he was actively engaged in preaching and in debate he felt that his doings were worthy of mention. When, on the other hand, he was not personally struggling for the truth it seemed to him that the events of his own life were of little importance. Of his suffering in the galleys, for example, he says very little, recalling only a few incidents where his personal conduct seemed to have some place in the divine plan. Of his early life he says nothing and only incidentally does he inform us as to his origin. When, in 1562, Mary's Bothwell sought his aid towards a reconciliation with Arran he replied to the earl that he had 'a good mynd to your house ... For, my Lord, my grandfather, goodsher and father, have served your

Lordshipis predecessoris, and some of thame have died under thair standartis; and this is a part of the obligatioun of our Scotishe kyndnes . . .' His family, he claimed, were dependents of Hepburn of Hailes whose hereditary castle was within a few miles of Haddington. He was a Lothian man and it may be remarked in passing that the contemporary English account of the expedition to Pinkie mentions the capture, not far from Haddington, of a comical Scotsman whose name was 'Knockes'. He may have been a kinsman of the reformer, and the point is of some interest because a seventeenth-century biographer of Knox (David Buchanan, 1644) alleged that his hero was closely connected with the gentle house of Knox of Ranfurly, near Paisley.

The little which Knox tells us of himself is confirmed by his first biographer, Theodore Beza, who included a picture and a brief life in the *Icones* of Protestant champions which he published in 1580. According to him Knox was *Giffordiensis* – Giffordgate is a suburb of Haddington – and since he is said to have died at the age of fifty-seven in 1572 he must have been born in 1515. From other evidence it is certain that Beza was supplied with both the picture and some biographical material by Scotsmen who had known Knox personally, and his story seems well founded, though one of his authorities, Sir Peter Young, said that Knox was fifty-nine when he died. In Arabic numerals the figures seven and nine might easily be confused and Knox may have been born in 1513. Beza goes on to say that he studied under John Major at St Andrews and bade fair to rival his master in sophistry; that he was driven into criticism by the reading of Jerome and Augustine and, as a consequence, was compelled to take refuge with John Cockburn of Ormiston. From Ormiston he issued a statement of his faith which caused Cardinal Beaton to strip him of his priesthood and condemn him for heresy, but he was preserved by the protection of Douglas of Longniddry. This brief account contains obvious misconceptions; Longniddry was not, as Beza supposed, a very powerful noble, and there is no mention elsewhere of the condemnation of Knox by Beaton; but it may be essentially true.

Archbishop Spottiswoode in his *History of the Church and State in Scotland,* said that Knox was sixty-seven when he died; the rash David Buchanan did the subtraction sum and boldly declared in the *Life,* which prefaced his edition of Knox's works, that Knox was born in 1505. He did not see the consequence of his assertion, and neither did any other biographer till David Laing, in 1846, issued the first volume of what is still the standard edition of Knox's works. Well aware that boys in the sixteenth century went up to the university at a very early age, and influenced, perhaps, by the alleged connection with Ranfurly, Laing held that Knox must have been educated at the university of Glasgow, where John Major taught between 1518 and 1523. The discovery of the name 'Johannes Knox' amongst the incorporates of 1522 supported this opinion, the more since the only 'John Knox' upon the St Andrews' roll was incorporated in 1571.

1505 was confidently assumed to be the birth year of Knox until 1905, when the proposal to celebrate the four-hundredth anniversary of Knox's birth stirred into activity doubts which had long existed in the mind of Hay Fleming. To him it seemed improbable that a man born in the Lothian (an archdeaconry of St Andrews) should seek his education anywhere else than in St Andrews; and it was obvious, he thought, that in the career of Knox St Andrews played a far greater part than did Glasgow. When the examination of an original manuscript of Spottiswoode's *History* gave his age as fifty-seven, not sixty-seven, the cautious critic concluded that, in all probability, Knox was born about 1514 or 1515.

Hay Fleming's view is generally accepted, though he himself was too good a scholar to be unaware that it presented difficulties. As Hume Brown had pointed out, George Buchanan, who was born near Glasgow, went to St Andrews because Major was there; and for the same reason Knox, who was born near Haddington, might have attended Glasgow. Again, Catholic controversialists made much of the fact that Knox was a very old man when he married his second wife, Margaret Stewart of Ochiltree, in 1564, and all contemporary writers agree that he was in extreme decreptitude when he died in 1572. In reply it can be urged that to the sixteenth century forty-nine might seem a considerable age, especially when the bride was a girl of sixteen or seventeen, and that Knox's health, obviously never very robust, must have been shaken by his experience in the galleys.

On the balance of the evidence the safer conclusion seems to be that Knox was educated at St Andrews and that he studied with success. It is certain that he was a priest in Haddington in 1540 and that he acted as a notary for some years. He must, therefore, have been an active man of thirty when he joined himself to Wishart's company; and though there is some ground to suppose that his knowledge of Greek was less than he pretended when he mocked the Catholic disputants for their ignorance about *agape*, it is evident that he was well instructed in Latin and in the dialectic which was so prominent in the scholastic training of that time. That he had conspicuous gifts appears from his career.

He was saved from sharing Wishart's fate by the action of his master, who dismissed him with the words 'one is sufficient for one sacrifice', and he became tutor to the sons of Hugh Douglas of Longniddry. In that service he remained until fear of persecution drove him, about easter 1547, into the castle of St Andrews, where Beaton's assassins were still holding out, partly because they held Arran's son as a hostage, partly because the Scottish gunnery was ineffective. A curious truce prevailed during which the 'Castilians' went freely into the city and Knox was able to teach in the parish church as well as in the castle chapel. Before long he was summoned, from the pulpit, by John Rough (who had begun as a friar and was to end as a martyr at Smithfield in 1557), himself to exercise the office of preacher. He burst into tears, but he could not refuse the call and thereafter distinguished himself in debates against the Catholic clergy.

Either because of his eminence in this matter, or because of his undistinguished birth, he was, unlike some of his fellow-captives, doomed to the galleys when the castle fell, in contravention, as he asserts, of the terms of surrender; and in the galleys he remained until he was freed in February 1549, at the instance of England, then moving towards peace with France. Normally the galleys were laid up in winter and his durance cannot have been uniformly severe, for he was able to revise a Lutheran tract, a treatise on Justification, written by Henry Balnaves, who was confined at Rouen, and he was able to communicate with others of his fellow prisoners, assuring them that in the end they would all be free. Yet his existence was miserable enough; he nearly died at sea when the galleys returned a second time to Scotland, though, as he recorded with pride, he was still able to predict that he would live to preach once more in the church of St Andrews, whose steeple he could behold from the waves.

Knox in England

On his liberation he found refuge and advancement in the Protestant England of Edward VI. He was appointed to be a licensed preacher, first at Berwick (April 1549) and later at Newcastle (1551). Whilst in the north he made the acquaintance of Mrs Elizabeth Bowes, daughter of Roger Aske and wife of Richard Bowes, captain of Norham castle, who was a Bowes of Streatlam and brother to Sir Robert Bowes, Warden of the Marches, and to Sir Ralph Bowes, knighted at Flodden. Mrs Bowes took Knox to be her spiritual adviser and Knox paid court to her daughter Marjory, whom he afterwards married. In all likelihood the betrothal was promoted by the pious mother, who was an heiress in her own right; but it gave great offence to her gentle kin.

There is no need to doubt Knox's assertion that his preaching did much to reduce turbulent Berwick to order, but the fact

that, in April 1550, he was summoned before Cuthbert Tunstall, Bishop of Durham, to explain his doctrine, signalizes a
matter of great importance. Knox in fact was one of the many
foreign Protestants who flocked into England in the days of
Edward, and who were persuading the deliberate Cranmer to
advance further and more swiftly than he meant to go. To these
vigorous reformers the First Prayer Book of 1549, which
Gardiner could accept, was still clogged with the superstitions
of popery, and great efforts were made to guide the English
church into a better way. The views of the forward party com-
mended themselves to the ambitious Northumberland, who
saw no hope in Mary and Spain, and in 1551 Knox was
appointed one of the six royal chaplains. Next year he was
brought south, perhaps to remove him further from the Scottish
border, ostensibly to deal with the Anabaptists, but also to be
a whetstone to quicken the Archbishop. There was a proposal,
supported, as Knox afterwards alleged, by Cecil, to give him
the see of Rochester; but if the offer was formally made he
refused it, and as he publicly compared the Duke of Northumberland to Achitophel and the Marquess of Winchester to
Shebna, it is little wonder that he was found 'neither grateful
nor pleasable'. He was twice summoned before the privy
council, the second time, perhaps, because he refused the living
of All Hallows in Bread Street; but though disliked by Northumberland, he still had influence, and it was largely at his
insistence that there was added to the Second Prayer Book of
Edward VI the famous Black Rubric which explained that to
receive the Communion kneeling did not involve adoration.

Knox's attitude to Northumberland may be held to show
self-interest in that he declined to trust his fortunes to a regime
which could not last. More justly may it be said to reveal
political wisdom simple, but profound; professions of extreme
piety by men who were bad were not to be trusted, and according to Knox's standards Northumberland was bad. To him the
fall of the wicked duke must have seemed a just dispensation of
providence and, like other people in England, he may have

hoped for a short time that Mary would not prove a persecutor. He remained preaching at Amersham (a little market town in Buckinghamshire), whither he had withdrawn after his trouble with the council, until the end of July, but he was in London to witness Mary's triumphal entry. On 22 December he was at Newcastle, and it was only in March 1554 that he crossed the sea.

Knox on the Continent, 1554-9

Arrived at Dieppe with ten groats for all his wealth he paused only to complete *A Godly Letter of Warning or Admonition to the Faithful in London, Newcastle and Berwick*, and set off for Switzerland; there he had discussions with Calvin at Geneva and Bullinger at Zurich, in an attempt to resolve his mind as to the attitude a true Christian should adopt towards an idolatrous prince. He returned to Dieppe in May to find that in England Mary was contemplating the marriage with Philip, and that in Scotland Mary of Guise had assumed the regency in the name of her daughter who was not yet twelve years old – 'als seimlye a sight', he thought, '(yf men had eis) as to putt a sadill upoun the back of ane unrewly kow.'

From Geneva he soon accepted a call to Frankfurt, where a congregation of English refugees had been allowed by the magistrates to worship in a church assigned to Vallerand Pullain and the French Protestants; but from this charge he was soon ousted by a fresh influx of Englishmen led by Richard Cox, afterwards Bishop of Ely. The newcomers wished to use the English Prayer Book, and it would have been easy for Knox to prevent their intrusion, unless they undertook to abandon it, on the ground that they proposed to depart far from the French form; but he, confident as ever in his own rightness, made no scruple in admitting them. Once admitted, however, the newcomers outvoted Knox, raised a clamour that his *Faithful Admonition* contained animadversions on Mary which the

Emperor must resent, and scared the magistrates into dismiss-
ing him from the city in March 1555.

He returned to Geneva, where Calvin, now in full control,
was establishing a discipline entirely to his mind, but though
he resumed his ministerial labours he soon set off to Scotland, perhaps on the summons of Mrs Bowes, perhaps because
he felt that the situation there was more promising than had
seemed likely.

The position of the Protestants had now become markedly
easier. To Knox this seemed a result of the inscrutable wisdom
of God, who turned the wicked purposes of 'Sathan' to his
own ends – the accession of 'mischevous Mary of the Spaniard's
blood' had had the effect of driving into Scotland leaders of
the new faith like William Harlaw, simple and devout, and
John Willock, educated and experienced. The truth is that
Mary of Guise, anxious to establish her authority in the
interests of France, found herself opposed by the Hamiltons,
whose head, the Earl of Arran (given the title of Duc de Châtelhérault, the revenues of which proved hard to secure), she had
displaced from the office of governor. As John Hamilton, the
duke's half-brother, was Archbishop of St Andrews, the regent
could place no great reliance upon the Scottish church, and,
indeed, whilst showing herself charming and complacent to all,
she took no decisive action against the Protestants until her
daughter was safely married to the Dauphin on 24 April 1558.
After the burning of Adam Wallace in the summer of 1550
there was no execution for heresy in Scotland till the aged
Walter Mill was burned at St Andrews in April 1558. Knox,
therefore, when he came to Scotland in the autumn of 1555,
enjoyed an astonishing impunity. He taught in Edinburgh,
discussed the propriety of bowing down in the house of
Rimmon with a group of influential men, and moved freely
about in Scotland preaching and ministering the Sacrament.
Although the scandalized clergy summoned him to appear at
the Blackfriars Church in Edinburgh on 15 May 1556, 'that
dyet held not' because his adherents, led by Erskine of Dun,

convened in great force. Knox, who had appeared in Edinburgh, remained there for ten days, preaching to greater congregations than ever in the Bishop of Dunkeld's great lodging. Emboldened by the interest shown by some of the nobles, he sent a letter to the Queen Dowager by the hand of Glencairn, evidently in the hope of making a convert; and he was probably cut to the quick when the lady handed it with a jest to the Bishop of Glasgow – 'please you my Lord to read a pasquil'. He left Scotland in July only at the urgent request of the English congregation in Geneva which had chosen him as minister; and when, after his departure, he was condemned and burned in effigy he replied by composing an *Appellation to the Nobility and Estates of Scotland*, which was published only in 1558. In Geneva he remained as minister of the congregation until the autumn of 1557, when, rather hesitantly, as it seems, he moved in response to letters from Scotland and came to Dieppe. He arrived on 24 August, only to find letters of a very different tenor awaiting him and either because of them or because the Spanish victory of St Quentin on 10 August had confused the situation, he abandoned his enterprise and returned once more to Geneva. He denied, even to himself, that his retreat was occasioned by fear, and it was, perhaps, dictated by political considerations, which he attributed to the guidance of God; but his very discussion of motives indicates an uneasy conscience, and it was in the resultant bitterness of mind that he began to write *The First Blast of the Trumpet against the Monstrous Regiment of Women*. The second and third blasts which had been prepared were never sounded; the first did damage enough to the trumpeter. The book was printed only in 1558 and in November of that year Bloody Mary died, to be succeeded by the godly Elizabeth. Knox, in his later dealings with Elizabeth and his own Queen Mary, tried to temper his conclusions by references to Deborah, but neither princess ever forgave him.

As a result rather of his own experience than of the discussions he had with other Protestant leaders, Knox had suffered some change in his political opinions during his period upon the Continent. Neither Calvin nor Bullinger had encouraged the view that armed resistance to an ungodly prince was the simple duty of good Christians, and when, in 1554, Knox sent his *Comfortable Epistle to the Afflicted Church of Christ* he warned his readers not to be 'revengers' in their own cause, but to leave vengeance to God. Only a few weeks later, however, in *A Faithful Admonition to the Professors of God's Truth in England* he prayed that God would, 'for His great mercies sake, stirre up some Phinees, Helias or Jehu, that the bloude of abhominable idolaters maye pacifie Goddes wrath . . .' This was a direct incitement to tyrannicide, and while, in his later works, the writer was, as a rule, less explicit, he evidently subscribed to the doctrine that rebellion against an ungodly 'magistrate' was entirely justifiable. Any hope he had had of an accommodation with the Queen Regent vanished when she sneered at his 'pasquil', and it is just possible that the discouraging letters which he received at Dieppe in October 1557 were due to the belief among the Protestant nobles that he would be an embarrassing ally. In the following December, it is true, some of them, including Argyll, Glencairn, Morton, Lorne (Argyll's son), and Erskine of Dun were constrained to unite themselves by the first formal 'Covenant' binding the 'haill congregation of Christ' to wage war against 'the congregatioun of Sathan'; but some politic heads may still have hoped that they could drive the Queen Mother to make terms. Hence the year 1558 was passed in an uneasy truce in which, even after Mary's marriage to the Dauphin was completed, the Protestants showed themselves confident if not aggressive; in Edinburgh itself the great procession of St Giles on 1 September was broken up by a disorderly mob. Knox, in his *History*, represents that the action of the crowd was spontaneous, but from that account itself the reader may infer some prearrangement. As the Covenant was obviously an instrument for war, and as the conferences of Marcoing and Cercamp in 1558 presaged the union of the Catholic powers in the peace of

Cateau-Cambrésis of April 1559, it may seem to us today that an open breach was inevitable; but this did not occur till, on 10 May 1559, the Queen Regent outlawed the Protestant preachers for 'non-compearance' at Stirling, although she had solemnly promised, under Protestant pressure, to delay their trial. Next day the religious houses of Perth were sacked by the mob, and although Knox alleges, in one place, that the disorders were the action of 'the raschall multitude', he also says that 'the spoile was permitted to the poore' as if the leaders had had the power to prevent it, and in a private letter he attributes the deed to the brethren.

Knox in the Crisis of 1559–60

Knox should have known the truth of the matter, for he himself was on the spot. Whether he was definitely summoned or whether he smelled the battle from afar when the trumpets sounded to Armageddon is not known; but he came to Edinburgh on 2 May and hurried off to Dundee and so to Perth. It may be presumed, though it is not certain, that he was one of the preachers whose denunciation of idolatry stirred up the final outbreak. After some hollow negotiations about Perth the 'Congregation' advanced fairly rapidly to Edinburgh, which they occupied on 29 June; on 26 July they were driven out, but though they returned again, with the assistance of the Hamiltons, and 'deposed' the Queen Mother on 21 October, their triumph was short-lived. Reinforced by French troops, who, in the general alarm, brought their wives with them, Mary fortified Leith, and early in November the Congregation abandoned the capital once more. They halted for a while at Stirling; but d'Oysel, the French ambassador, following up his advantage, swooped upon them there, cut their forces in two, drove the westerners home in dismay and followed the others up along the north shore of the Firth of Forth. Fighting valiantly, the reformers were driven east; the French established a base at Kinghorn opposite Leith; the Lord James with his friends girded himself for the defence of St Andrews. On 23 January, however, English ships appeared in the Firth and cut the supply lines of the French, who sullenly withdrew over the country they had wasted in their advance. Scottish negotiators went to Holy Island; on 27 February a contract was concluded between James, Duke of Châtelhérault as second person in Scotland and Thomas, Duke of Norfolk, Earl Marshal of England, for the expulsion of the French forces. An English army appeared early in April. Leith defended itself manfully, but the death of the Queen Regent on 11 June weakened the cause of France, and on 6 July was signed the treaty of Leith or Edinburgh, between England and France, to which certain important sections dealing with the affairs of Scotland were appended.

The essential points were that while Mary and Francis were acknowledged to be sovereigns in Scotland they were to renounce and cease to use the arms of England; that French troops were to withdraw altogether from Scotland; that the Scots might summon a Parliament and arrange a provisional government of twelve members of whom Mary should appoint seven out of a list of twenty-four prepared by the estates. The effect was to leave power in the hands of the Protestant party, though it was provided that the parliament was not to make decisions on matters of religion, but only prepare proposals to be submitted to the Queen and her husband.

In all the stirring movement of the revolution Knox played a conspicuous part. His was the voice which incited to the 'purgation' of St Andrews by preaching (on 11 June 1559) upon the ejection of the traders from the temple of Jerusalem, and which, when all was going ill, proclaimed an undying confidence in the great sermon preached at Stirling on 8 November 1559. His was the pen which drafted the various memorials in which the Congregation justified its actions on the ground, largely, of the double-dealing of the Queen Regent on the point of religion. The second book of his *History*, a *livre de circonstance* written in the heat of the action, sets forth his attitude of mind with clarity, or with seeming clarity. Yet it must be noted that in the justification, written in Latin, which the lords presented to the great world of politics, little is said of religion at all; there the *gravamen* is the attempt of Mary to turn Scotland into a province of France. That Knox was aware of the political aspect of the struggle is obvious. He knew that the lords had hoped for English help; he himself was in touch with Cecil, with whom he had communicated from Dieppe in April, as early as 19 July 1559; and for the rest of the year he was actively employed in soliciting English aid. 'In twenty-four hours', he wrote, 'I have not four free to naturall rest, and ease of this wicked carcass'. He strove awkwardly enough to pacify Elizabeth about the unfortunate *First Blast*; he constantly urged the sending of English troops, or at least English money; and when the Elizabethan government, not being at war with France, hesitated to act, he even proposed that a thousand or more men might be allowed to come as volunteers or even as denounced rebels. He was one of the emissaries sent to England early in 1560; but he turned out to be so maladroit a diplomatist that Sir James Crofts, captain of Berwick, sent him home on the ground that eloquent preachers were sorely needed in Scotland, and the negotiation was entrusted to others, among whom the able William Maitland of Lethington became conspicuous. When, at a later date, between 1564 and 1566, probably towards the end of 1565, Knox continued his history in what is now Book III, he was at no pains to conceal his political action, and included in his text some of his diplomatic correspondence.

How are we to account for the fact that in the original 'Book' of 1559–60, Knox represented the revolution as almost purely religious and said so little of the political issue which was emphasized by the protagonists of his party? It may fairly be supposed that he did not wish at the earlier date to disclose the negotiations with England (in fact his writing, though known to Randolph in September 1560, was not published till a much later date). Yet it is difficult to resist the conclusion that he wished to make the best case possible against Mary of Guise and that he felt safest upon the ground of religion. In support of this view it may be urged that either he was not fully apprised of the actions of his leaders or that he glossed them over. His version, for example, of the 'Appointment' made at Leith on 24 July 1559, when the Congregation abandoned Edinburgh for the first time, is rather curious. He states plainly the *desiderata* of the Congregation, which included the condition that the Mass should not be re-introduced into any place where it was then suppressed; with equal clarity he sets forth the arrangement actually made which does not include this clause; he then prints a proclamation made by his own party which does include it. The discrepancy between the two versions he explains away on the ground that the 'alteration in words and order was made without the knowledge and consent of those whose counsel we had used in all cases before'. From the context this appears to mean that some persons other than Knox and his friends had signed the agreement on behalf of the Congregation; that Knox unconcernedly regarded their action as invalid, and that he accused the Queen Mother of treachery in that she did not keep an agreement which had not, in fact, been made. His ignorance or disingenuousness with regard to the Protestant mobs has already been noted. Plainly, book two, in its original form, was a party pamphlet, and it was possible for Andrew Lang in *John Knox and the Reformation in Scotland* to argue that it was not the Queen Mother but the Congregation which practised deceit.

For Knox it must be said that if he 'dressed' his facts for his *livre de circonstance* he did not depart seriously from the truth as he knew it. For him the religious issue was the essential issue. It must be added that fundamentally he was quite right. There was a real intention to bring Scotland completely under the control of France; Mary of Guise was merely driving time; her fixed purpose was to promote the interests of her house, which, even more than the royal house of Valois, was devoted to the Roman Catholic cause. Mary may not have been personally cruel and dishonest – even Knox's account, in spite of its vituperation, endows her with charm – but she was single-minded in her cause, and Knox, who thought that her cause was of the devil, strove to suppress it with every means within his power. His effort was successful. Granted that political and economic factors operated on his side, it is certain that it was his own fierce energy which held his party together in the evil day and contributed greatly to the final success. As Randolph said of him 'the voice of one man is able, in an hour, to put more life in us, than six hundred trumpets continually blustering in our ears'. Mention has been made already (p.143) of the potency of Knox's preaching and indeed one of his greatest weapons was his eloquence.

Our own age, when the sound of the human voice can be produced mechanically, is apt to overlook the hour of oratory. Other ages had more respect for it. Indeed the Greek word for eloquence was *deinotas*, which also meant 'terribleness'; but we need not go back to Demosthenes or forward to Gladstone (whose early successes have been attributed to his oratory in a recent appraisal). If we confine ourselves to Knox we have only to read aloud one of his perorations to realize the power of a resolute conviction expressed in telling words.

The Revolution Settlement, 1560

The settlement made by the triumphant revolutionaries reveals both the underlying spirit and the creative hand of Knox. The Parliament promised by the treaty of Leith duly met on 1 August. An attempt was made both then and later to deny its competence upon technical grounds, but this Knox brushed contemptuously aside – 'that we litill regarded, or yit do regarde'. For him, evidently, the revolution was a law unto itself. Touching the manner of holding Parliament he had, in fact, little to defend; but the application of his argument to the work done by Parliament was far less defensible. The treaty of Leith had plainly provided that no decision on ecclesiastical matters was to be taken without reference to Mary and Francis, but the Parliament boldly effected a complete revolution in ecclesiastical affairs. It at once began to consider a *Confession of Faith* which was passed clause by clause in the face of a very feeble protest by a few bishops, and on 17 August was ratified in its entirety. A week later the whole foundations of the Roman church in Scotland were swept away by three acts passed on a single day: the authority of the Pope was abolished; all acts not in conformity with the Confession were abrogated; the Sacraments were reduced to two and the celebration of Communion, except in the Protestant fashion, was made punishable by a gradation of penalties culminating in death for the third offence. As compared with the almost contemporary English settlement there were both differences and resemblances. Whereas the English Act of Uniformity enforced the use of one form of public worship the Scots were content to condemn only one religious rite, the Mass. In fact, the *Book of Common Order,* used by Knox's congregation in Geneva, was generally introduced and, with its accompanying version of the Psalms, remained the accepted standard in Scotland until the *Directory of Public Worship,* made by the Westminster Assembly, was established in 1645. It may be noted in passing that this *Book of Common Order,* though often called the Geneva Book, was founded upon a manner of service used by the congregation at Frankfurt, and that it was itself rather a directory than a set form.

Again, while the English Act of Supremacy endowed the Crown with most of the privileges taken from the Pope, the Scottish Act stopped short with the abrogation of papal power. The *Book of Discipline,* prepared by Knox and his friends, provided for an independent church whose authority was rooted in congregations made wise by the Word of God. But this *Book of Discipline,* though at first a good number of nobles and gentry subscribed to it, was never accepted by the

Parliament of 1560 or by any other Parliament, and remained an ideal. Maitland of Lethington said in 'mockage': 'We mon now forget our selffis, and beir the barrow to buyld the housses of God'; the Protestant politicians had not overthrown Rome to endow a pack of enthusiastic ministers, and to them the aspirations of Knox were 'devote imaginationis'. The Presbyterian church which eventually emerged in Scotland found its constitution and its machinery only by slow development.

Both the *Confession of Faith* and the *Book of Discipline* were prepared by a committee of six ministers, the 'Six Johns' (Winram, Spottiswoode, Willock, Douglas, Row, and Knox), and throughout both the absolute conviction and the driving force of Knox are evident. The *Confession of Faith*, though it owes something to John à Lasco and even something to Luther, is in the main Calvinist. It begins with first principles – with God and the creation of man; it then explains how Adam and Eve transgressed, and how 'the image of God was utterly defaced in man' who could be redeemed from the ensuing bondage to Satan only by 'the power of the Holy Ghost working in the hearts of the elect of God'. While the *Confession* takes the essential kirk to be a mystical body of all ages, nations, and tongues, invisible, known only to God and containing the kirk triumphant as well as the kirk militant, it goes on to set forth the 'notes' by which a true kirk could always be distinguished – the true preaching of the word, the right administration of the Sacrament, and ecclesiastical discipline uprightly administered. (The same *criteria*, it may be observed, are set forth in the famous *Admonition* presented to Elizabeth's Parliament in 1572.) The obvious difficulty involved in the use of the words 'true' and 'right' is met by the assertion that true doctrine is to be found in the Scriptures interpreted on the assumption that the Holy Spirit could never contradict itself, and that the actual sayings and doings of Christ would provide a constant standard. Plainly the ministers, who were not only the proper interpreters of the Word, but the proper administrators of the Sacraments, were given great power; and the section on the

'Civil Magistrat', while magnifying royal authority, limits it by the *caveat* that this authority must be used to promote good and redress evil.

The effect of the *Confession* was therefore to establish an authority outside of that of the state, and as this authority lay in the hands of the kirk as the interpreter of God's will, it was obviously necessary to explain at full length the fabric of an organization which could truly interpret the Scriptures, rightly administer the Sacraments, and justly uphold ecclesiastical discipline. The attempt was made in the *Book of Discipline*. Proceeding on the assumption that the wealth of the secular clergy of the old church should go to the new kirk, the book provided for the establishment of ministers throughout Scotland and for the erection of a national system of education; it also made some suggestions, undeveloped, for the relief of poverty. The minister, whose work was the essential feature of the whole structure, could be appointed only after a process of election, examination, and admission, and it was by the congregation that he was to be elected. Because this was so, and because the minister was always subject, in some degree, to the censure of his flock, it was absolutely necessary for the congregation to be properly educated. To that end was devised a magnificent system of elementary and secondary schools and well organized universities controlled by examinations and certificates in the modern way. Young people who showed themselves not to be book-minded were to be trained to a craft, but every child, rich or poor, was to have the fullest opportunity.

Realizing that some time must elapse before a sufficient number of ministers could be found, the authors of the book provided for 'readers' who might do parochial work under supervision, and for 'superintendents' who should, besides ministering each in his own kirk, ride round and oversee the working of the church in the adjacent districts. The office of superintendent was apparently copied from a Danish model. These superintendents were to be well paid. As the ten areas assigned to them represented a sensible readjustment of the old dioceses, and as Knox, at the end of his life, was prepared to accept the 'Tulchan' bishops erected by Morton,* it has been argued that he was not opposed to episcopacy. Too much has been made of this. It is a matter of terms. Knox, though not very learned in Greek, must have known that *episcopos* meant 'overseer', and in that sense would recognize that 'superintendents' might well be useful in an unformed church. His superintendents, however, were under the censure of their subordinates; like ministers they could be elected and deposed; the 'Apostolic Succession' was categorically rejected; and if Knox's comments on the 'Tulchan' establishment be regarded it will be seen that he, broken in health, was accepting what he could not prevent, and was endeavouring to make sure that the state should not obtain complete control over the kirk. It must be added that Knox himself never endeavoured to become a bishop, and the argument that he found himself more influential and very well paid as minister of St Giles is hardly good. Knox was by nature a master, and if he had thought that episcopacy contained any essential mastery in the kirk he would himself have become a bishop.

Knox's influence on the Wane

The rejection of the *Book of Discipline* by the Estates in January 1561 was a serious blow to the power of Knox, and with the return of Mary from France in the following August his influence began slowly to wane. The Queen's proclamation, issued on 25 August, promised not to attempt anything against the form of religion she found established on her arrival, and it is possible to suppose from Knox's own words that even his

---

* A *Tulchan* was a calf's skin stuffed with straw and set beside a cow to encourage her to give milk. The 'bishops' erected by Morton after 1572 had the title, but were compelled to surrender much of the revenue to government pensioners.

criticism was for the moment disarmed. None the less, when the Queen introduced her private Mass into Holyrood House he boldly declared in a sermon that one Mass was more fearful to him than if ten thousand armed enemies were landed to suppress the whole religion; but though the English agent Randolph asserted that Knox 'rulethe the roste, and of hym all men stande in feare', yet even he doubted lest the preacher's thunderings from the pulpit would one day 'marre all'. Compromise was in the air, and the young Queen, aware that Knox still spoke to a large public from the pulpit of St Giles, endeavoured to lure him from his opposition by the exercise of her personal charm. To that end she summoned him to the first of the famous interviews in September 1561, and later offered him the privilege of coming to admonish her privately whenever he thought fit. The idea that he thrust himself upon his mistress and reduced her to tears with his contumelious words is false. Mary wept only on one occasion and then in irritation (not unjustifiable) at Knox's attempts to prevent her marriage with a Catholic prince. On that occasion he was summoned to be rebuked; later he was brought before the Queen and Council to be charged with treason on the ground that he had convoked the Queen's lieges on his own authority in order to defend two brethren who had opposed the use of the Mass. Knox was saved by his friends, but he was in no case to bully the Queen; he had become an embarrassment to his own party.

The Catholics were, of course, against him; and they were probably right in their belief that the young Queen would show herself upon their side. On their hostility Knox must obviously have reckoned all along; what destroyed his authority was the attitude of his own party. In it were many men, notably the Queen's half-brother the Lord James and the subtle Maitland of Lethington, who believed that Mary must, for her own sake, implement the promise made in the proclamation of 25 August. To the politicians it appeared that Mary's interest in the English crown had now become a diplomatic card of the first importance. She declined to ratify the treaty of Leith on the ground that her envoys had exceeded their instructions; and although formally this was not so, it is obvious that she had a real grievance in that the treaty was so worded as to make her renounce her right to the English crown 'in all times coming'. There seemed room for a bargain whereby Mary should abandon her present pretensions in return for an acknowledgement that she was Elizabeth's heir. Such an arrangement proved impossible since the English Queen refused to 'pin up her winding sheet before her eyes' by naming a successor; but it was under discussion for some time, and it gained a significance because, as early as 1562, there were rumours that Elizabeth would never bear a child. Elizabeth, for her part, was not anxious for a definite quarrel with a princess who might marry a powerful Catholic prince, perhaps even Don Carlos, and become the spearhead of a grand Catholic attack upon schismatic England. Accordingly she too endeavoured to guide the steps of Mary towards moderation in religion and, incidentally, towards some undistinguished husband.

In these circumstances neither the politic Protestants of Scotland nor the English were minded to ally with Knox, who believed that all Catholics were striving against God and that the charming Queen in her pretence of tolerating Protestantism was no more sincere than her mother had been. He admitted the 'inchantment whereby men are bewitched' but he did not fall a victim. From his naive account of the interviews it may be deduced that he believed himself to have combined courtly grace with directness of speech, and also that he thought himself the winner of the dialectic battle. To some modern readers it may appear that Mary had the better of the encounter, since she forced her redoubtable opponent to admit that he relied upon his own interpretation of the Scriptures; but if the woman had the victory in logic it was the man who was right in instinct. Neither as a Catholic nor as an authoritarian could Mary compromise with Protestantism and the assertion that subjects could control their prince. Part of her seeming complacence was, no doubt, due to her desire to please and her love of the 'joyusitie' in which she had been bred, but part of it was certainly due to political considerations; she was biding her time. Knox, the unconvinced, was an embarrassment to the politicians. He quarrelled definitely with the Lord James, now Earl of Moray, to whom he did not speak or write for a long time; and though he met with Lethington in 1564 it was only to dispute about the rights of princes. In all the negotiations with England at this time he played no part at all.

Whilst he thus dropped out of politics he was unable to call an organized kirk to his aid. The *Book of Discipline* remained an empty dream; by an act of the Privy Council of February 1562, the existing holders of church lands and revenues – by no means all clerics – were to retain two-thirds of their income, the remaining third to go to the Crown which was charged with the obligation of paying the ministers. 'I see', said Knox, 'Twa partis freely gevin to the Devill, and the Third maun be divided betwix God and the Devill.' As late as 1567 there were only two hundred and fifty-seven ministers for one thousand and eighty churches, along with six hundred and six 'readers' and 'exhorters'; and only slowly did the organization grow. The Kirk Session was there from the start. At the other end of the hierarchy the General Assembly made its appearance in 1560. This was, at first, an uncertain body; its first meeting contained only forty-two members of whom thirty-six were laymen; to begin with it was a biennial affair, meeting every year at the height of summer and again in the depth of winter; and only in 1563 did a 'moderator' make a somewhat tentative appearance. The Synod, or Provincial Assembly, was introduced in 1562, but the Presbytery Court, founded from a group of parishes, was not introduced until 1580, and even then owed much to an English model.

This slow and uncertain development at once reveals and explains the relative impotence of Knox. He was still of great reputation; in 1564 he married Margaret Stewart of Ochiltree, the daughter of one of his supporters Lord Ochiltree, to the derision of his Catholic critics. Nicol Burne described him as riding to his wedding with a great court on a trim gelding not like a prophet or old decrepit priest as he was, but like a prince of the blood with his taffeta ribbons, gold rings, and jewels. Knox may have looked older than his age and his enemies attributed his conquest to sorcery.

In the dramatic crises of Mary's reign during the years 1566–67 Knox played little part. Though he was not old his health was feeble; but it may have been uncertainty of mind as well as bodily weakness which withheld him from the action. His principles, indeed, remained unaltered. Rome remained the great and soul-destroying work of the devil, and Mary, to whom he did not hesitate to give a very evil name, was a worthy agent of the great 'whore of Babylon'. But some of his friends had disappointed him, of others he was uncertain, and in the place of the old sureness of action there appears a degree of hesitancy. Occasionally, however, he showed himself resolute enough. When Darnley, anxious to placate the opinion of Edinburgh, attended a service at St Giles in August 1565 (just when Moray and his friends were mustering against the Queen), Knox in his sermon, which was very long, showed how 'God justly punished Ahab and his posterity, because he would not take order with that harlot Jezebel'. Not surprisingly, he was summoned before the Council, where he appears to have been more outspoken than ever, warning Mary that her husband would be an instrument of her ruin; and he suffered no penalty save that he was forbidden to preach for fifteen or twenty days.

After the Queen had ejected her rebels his position must have become hazardous and, perhaps in his own interest, he was sent out of Edinburgh on an indeterminate mission to visit the churches of the south; after the murder of Riccio, in which he seems to have had no part at all, he was in real peril and early in 1566 he betook himself to Kyle, where he found occupation in completing and polishing his *History*. Although he returned to Edinburgh in September 1556, when, presumably, the birth of Prince James had slackened the tension, he soon got leave from the General Assembly to visit the two sons of his first marriage.*

The Last Years of Knox, 1567-72

Only upon the fall of Mary did he return to his own land. In July 1567, he was threatening the people with the great plague of God if she were not 'condignly punished'. On 29 July he preached at the coronation of James and in the following December, at the opening of a 'Protestant' Parliament, which ratified the acts of 1560. When the Queen escaped to England he still pursued her with his hate, warning Cecil that 'if ye strike not at the root the branches that appear to be broken will bud again', and his hate became more envenomed when his old patron, the Regent Moray, was murdered in the streets of Linlithgow in January, 1570. His old eloquence came to his aid and in the month following the murder he brought to tears a congregation of three thousand when he preached in St Giles on 'Blessed are the Dead that Die in the Lord'. Towards the end of 1570 he had a slight stroke, and in the following spring he was vexed by accusations launched from Edinburgh Castle where Kirkcaldy of Grange, once his own ally and a henchman of Moray, still held out for the Queen. His friends urged him to disregard the slanders, but he insisted in replying from the pulpit of St Giles to the charges of sedition, schism, and erroneous teaching, and concluded by giving him 'a lye in his throat, that either dar, or will say, that ever I socht support against my native countrie'.

In May 1571, he left Edinburgh for St Andrews. The famous account of his sojourn there given in James Melville's *Diary*

* Nathaniel and Eleazer, aged nine and eight respectively, who afterwards went to St John's College, Cambridge; the younger became a clergyman in the Church of England, and died in 1591. By his second wife he had three daughters, Martha, Margaret, and Elizabeth.

shows him as a 'done' man who had to be assisted into the pulpit, but who, in the course of his sermon, became so vigorous that he was 'lyke to ding that pulpit in blads and fly out of it'. He absolutely refused to take any part in the installation of John Douglas, rector of the university (whom he personally liked), as Archbishop of St Andrews, and heartily supported St Leonard's College in its dispute with St Salvator's, repudiating, incidentally, the allegation that he had signed the 'band' for the Darnley murder. Though unable to attend the General Assembly at Perth, he sent pertinent articles and questions about the 'Tulchan' establishment, with a covering letter containing the admonition 'above all things, preserve the church from the bondage of the universities'. He even found time to publish a reply, written long before, to the Jesuit James Tyrie. In that he makes mention of his approaching end; an appendix, dated 12 July 1572, concludes:

'I hartly salute and tak my good-night of all the faithfull in both the Realmes; earnestly desyring the assistance of their prayers, that without any notable sclander to the Evangell of Jesus Christ I may end my battell: for as the worlde is wearie of me, so am I of it.'

In all his correspondence of this period the same theme appears; it was high time that he was gone.

Yet it was not in St Andrews, but in Edinburgh that death came to him. His colleague in St Giles, John Craig, had shown himself too friendly to the party in the Castle and when, on 31 July, a truce was arranged, the congregation anxiously summoned their trusted minister to return to them. He left St Andrews on 17 August, and on the last day of the month occupied his pulpit once more. He was now very feeble. On 7 September he wrote to his chosen successor, James Lawson of Aberdeen, 'Haist, leist ye come to lait', and when October came his voice was audible only to those in his immediate vicinity. Still the indomitable will remained. When the news

of the St Bartholemew Day Massacre came he preached a
sermon against the King of France so vehement that the
French ambassador protested: in vain, for the Lords said
that they could not stop Knox from preaching even against
themselves. He consented, if Killigrew can be trusted, to the
plan for having Mary executed in Scotland; he warned Kirkcaldy that unless he repented he would be hanged on the
gallows facing the sun.

The Legacy of Knox to Scotland

Hanged that valiant and luckless captain was when Edinburgh
Castle surrendered to an Anglo-Scottish army on 28 May
1573; but long ere the prophecy was fulfilled its maker was
dead. On 9 November, Knox inducted Lawson into St Giles,
and two days later he took to his bed. The story of his last
hours shows him in a humane light; paying his servant his last
wages with a luck-penny and a grim joke; opening a hogshead
of wine for two callers, John Durie and Archibald Stewart, and
bidding Archibald send for the same so long as it lasted, 'for
he wald never tarie until it were drunken'; taking his last 'gud
nycht' of his elders and deacons, and making arrangements
about his coffin. To a pious woman who praised his godliness
he said, 'Ladie, flesch of itself is ower proude and neidis no
meanis to esteam the self'; and when he repeated the Lord's
Prayer he said 'who can pronunce so holie wordis?' He caused
his wife to read the fifteenth chapter of the first Epistle to the
Corinthians 'of the Resurrection', and then the place where
'first I caist my first ancre'. So she read the seventeenth chapter
of St John which deals with the eternal communion of the
Father, the Son and those whom God had given to the Son.
Soon afterwards he died as confident in the face of death as he
had been throughout his life.

The confidence that he was among those given by the Father
to the Son is the secret of Knox's strength and of his weakness,

too. Of his weakness he was conscious. In a prayer composed in March 1566, he wrote:

'In youth, myd age, and now, after many battelles, I find nothing into me bot vanitie and corruption. For, in quyetnes I am negligent, in trouble impatient, tending to disperation; and in the meane state, I am so caryed away with vane fantaseis, that, (allace), O Lord, they withdraw me from the presence of thy Majestie.'

Yet he went on to say, 'be thy meare grace I dout not myself to be electit to eternal salvation in Jesus Christ'. At one time, in and about the year 1565, he seems to have felt that the struggle had availed nought and that all his efforts had been vain. Yet as the bodily weakness, which had helped to produce the depression, increased, so did his spirit regain its strength, and as he drew near to death he felt a surge of exaltation. At the end of his controversy with the Marians in 1571 he was able to write:

'What I have bene to my cuntrie, albeit this unthankful aige will not knowe, yet the aiges to come wilbe compelled to beir witnes to the treuth.'

History has vindicated his opinion of himself. He was right in thinking that between the *semper eadem* of Rome and the spirit of Protestantism there could be no compromise; he was right in believing that Protestantism, if it was to establish itself, must do so by force and that, if it did, the Papacy would surely try by force to recover its lost dominions. From his assumption that the cause of Rome was the cause of evil it followed that for him there was, throughout his life, a constant battle between God and the devil, and from his certainty that he was on the side of God there followed the assurance that his side must ultimately prevail. He firmly believed and did not hesitate to assert that true ministers had the same power to remit sins

which Jesus granted to his apostles, and the *Book of Discipline*
demands that a congregation should obey its chosen minister
'evin as thai wald obey God Him self'. He believed that he had
himself the gift of prophecy. Hence came his power. Hence the
eloquence that fired the hearts of men and his obvious ascen-
dency over the hearts of women. His unshakable conviction
made him ruthless towards the enemies of truth as he knew it;
but it also made him indomitable in misfortune, and in the good
day and the evil day alike still constant to his purpose.

The form of religion which he, more than any one man,
erected in Scotland has seemed to many people ungracious and
hard, and by its very severity an easy prey to loud hypocrisy.
Yet it established the two ideas that every human act was of
eternal significance and that God demanded of all his creatures
absolute submission to His Will. Gentle and simple, rich and
poor, all were equal in the sight of God and all alike owed
obedience to the divine law. No man could fulfil the whole of
the law, but the Grace of God and the imputed righteousness
of Christ would come to the aid of those 'elected' – there was
the rub! – by God in His inscrutable wisdom, and the elect
would be known by their works. It was the duty of every man,
in obeying the Law of God, to turn to the use of the commonwealth whatever powers he possessed, to make full use of the
talent God had given him, and although all were equal in the
sight of God, in the world of men there was a great variety of
gifts. The ideal state of the *Book of Discipline* might be described in modern parlance as a 'welfare state', but it was not
egalitarian.

This *Book of Discipline*, though it was never authorized by
Parliament, moulded the life of Scotland for centuries. Certain
modern critics, who brand Knox as an iconoclast without great
consideration of the thing which he destroyed, say that it produced in Scotland a people self-righteous and narrow in religion, indifferent to the graces of life, blind to the holiness of
beauty, and deaf to all music save the Psalms. Others believe that
it was a great factor in producing a race patient of discipline,

valuing moral integrity, anxious for education, convinced of the dignity of honest work, trained to endeavour and to enterprise, apt for adventure and even for imperialism. Those who disparage Knox would do well to remember that in denouncing him they denounce also the qualities which have enabled the children of a small poor country to set their mark upon the history of the world.

BIBLIOGRAPHICAL NOTE

The Life of John Knox, by Thomas McCrie (2 vols., 1811 and several later editions); although called 'learned and unreadable' by R. L. Stevenson and although a frank admirer of Knox, McCrie was a good scholar, and his notes and appendices have been freely used by later biographers.

John Knox, by P. Hume Brown (2 vols., 1895), is still the standard biography. The author upheld Knox but was moderate in tone and was very well informed.

John Knox and the Reformation, by Andrew Lang (1905), a critical but not unfriendly examination of Knox and his career; defends Mary of Guise from Knox's charge of perfidy.

An Essay on *John Knox and his Relations to Women* is included in R. L. Stevenson's *Familiar Studies of Men and Books* (Edinburgh Edition, 1894–6).

John Knox, by Lord Eustace Percy (1937), gives a generous estimate of Knox. Particularly good for the formation of his political ideas between 1550 and 1559.

The Works of John Knox, edited David Laing (6 vols., 1846–64), is the standard edition.

The History of the Reformation in Scotland, edited W. Croft Dickinson (2 vols., 1949), presents the text in a rationalized form justified on the ground that the orthography of the standard edition is not sacrosanct since it represents the work of eight different scribes. The introduction and notes contain the best account of Knox and his works yet published.

Calendar of State Papers, Scotland, Elizabeth (vols. I to IV).

PART SIX

The Council of the North

THE COUNCIL OF THE NORTH

by

F. W. BROOKS

'The king, intending also the suppression of the greater Monasteries, which he effected in the 31st of his Reign, for the preventing of future Dangers and keeping those Northern Counties in Quiet, raised a President and Council at *York*, and gave them his several Powers and Authorities, under one great Seal of *Oyer and Terminer etc.* . . . which Court was continued till the Troubles of the King and Nation, in the time of Charles I.'

It is in these words quoted from Coke that Drake, the eighteenth-century historian of York, describes the foundation of the Council of the North in the year 1537, after the suppression of the Pilgrimage of Grace. But Drake was mistaken; the Council in the North was an older expedient to meet the even older problems of the north. In this, as in so many other directions, what were at one time thought to be Tudor innovations are now recognized as developments of existing institutions. Like the Star Chamber, its mightier counterpart, the Council of the North was a modification of a Yorkist or even a Lancastrian institution. Yet there is something of a half-truth in Drake's remarks. The year 1537 did witness the issue of a new commission for the better government of the north, and the Council of the North was indeed one of those bodies which can colourably be regarded as provincial offshoots of the Tudor Council.

At first sight it would seem that the Tudors, relying, as they did, on conciliar government, found it advisable to establish local replicas of the Council in the outlying parts of the kingdom. But, so far as the north was concerned, both the problem and the remedy were older than the Tudors.

That problem was acutely summed up by a man who knew what he was talking about – Robert Aske, the leader of the Pilgrimage of Grace. Presenting the ultimatum of the rebels to the leading men of the north at Pontefract Castle in 1536 he said, 'The profits of the abbeys suppressed, tenths and first fruits, went out of those (i.e. the north) parts. By occasion whereof, within short space of years, there should be no money or treasure in those parts, neither the tenant to have to pay his rents to the lord, nor the lord to have money to do the King service withal, for so much as in those parts was neither the presence of his grace, execution of his laws, nor yet but little recourse of merchandise, so that of necessity the said county should either "pratysh"* with the Scots, or of very poverty be forced to make commotions or rebellions.'

This emphasizes the chief troubles of the north, its remoteness, its poverty, its lawlessness and, above all, the fear and hatred of the Scots. It was this last point that really distinguished the five northern counties. Wales, the west, even East Anglia might be lawless; they were remote and some of them were poor, but none of them had to face the problems of a frontier province.

Here was the dilemma that confronted Lancastrians, Yorkists, and Tudors in turn. They had to defend the country against the ever vigilant foe to the north. They could only do so by raising a standing army, or by entrusting the defence of the frontier to the men of the frontier. But, if the frontier defence were left to the frontiersmen, what guarantee was there that they would not turn their arms against the government? No statesman at the end of the fifteenth century could have been sanguine. Percies, Scropes, Nevilles – all had at different times turned against their rulers. But the dilemma persisted. Henry VII, able statesman that he was, tried to escape it. Although he owed his victory at Bosworth as much to the Earl of Northumberland as to any man, he refused to renew his commission as Lord Warden of the Marches and put him in the Tower.

* i.e. make terms.

Within a few months, however, he realised that, to govern the north, he must have a Percy. So Northumberland was taken from the Tower and restored to his offices of Lord Warden of the East and Middle Marches. Ironically enough he met his death in a riot at Topcliffe when he was tax-collecting for Henry in 1489.

In the fourteenth century this problem of the north and the Scots had been met by the removal of the Court and the great offices of state to York. All three Edwards made York their capital for periods extending to several years. But the pre-occupation of Edward III with France broke the tradition, and a new system, that of the appointment of a Warden of the Marches, was evolved. But to put the whole control of the north in the hands of one man was to take a very considerable risk, and the March was therefore, after 1381, divided into the East, Middle and West Marches. But the authority of the warden was always curtailed by the existence of numerous liberties in the northern counties. Quite apart from such great franchises as the Bishopric of Durham and the Archbishop of York's Liberty of Hexham, there were scores of smaller ones. At the end of the fourteenth century, the Percies owned almost a hundred baronies and manors. In these, the warden and his officers had no jurisdiction except through the lord. If a fugitive escaped into a liberty, all that the warden could do was to demand that the lord should give him up and if the lord refused or procrastinated there was nothing the warden could do about it. Small wonder that, having failed to suppress the liberties, the Lancastrian and Yorkist rulers thought that the best solution was to take the greatest of the northern lords, the Percies and the Nevilles, into partnership. The relations of Henry IV and Henry V with the Percies are illuminating. Henry IV, who himself, as Duke of Lancaster, was a great northern magnate, with extensive estates in Yorkshire as well as Lancashire, obtained his throne with the help of the Percies. In 1403 they quarrelled with him, and the successive defeats of Hotspur at Shrewsbury and of Northumberland at Bramham Moor might be thought to have broken their power once and for all. Yet what do we find? In 1416 Henry Percy is exchanged out of Scotland, restored to his estates and made Warden of the East and Middle Marches, and this, in spite of, or perhaps because of, the Scrope conspiracy of 1415! The fact is that the Percies were indispensable for the government of the north.

Some authorities have seen in the wardens of the Marches and their council the germ of the later Council of the North, but it is fairly obvious that Dr Rachel Reid was right in denying this. There are certain very important differences. The authority of the warden was limited to the four northern counties and did not include Yorkshire. It also differed in character from that of the later Council. The authority of the warden is largely military. He can call out the local forces, enforce truces with the Scots, punish breaches of the truce, hand Scots malefactors to his opposite number, the Scotch Warden, and execute summary justice on English reivers taken or handed over by the Scots. Although, however, it may be true that the authority of the wardens was limited in this way, we must never lose sight of the fact that the authority of a Neville or Percy did not merely stem from his commission. He was a great magnate in his own right, and both families were pushing south from the late fourteenth century onwards, and obtaining vast estates and castles in Yorkshire. We instinctively connect the Percies with Alnwick and the Nevilles with Raby, but a fifteenth-century Percy was more likely to be found at Leconfield or Wressle in the East Riding, or Topcliffe in the Vale of York than at Alnwick, whilst the Nevilles watched their rivals from Middleham or Sheriff Hutton, both in the Vale of York. With estates went patronage. Henry, fourth Earl of Northumberland, could meet Henry VII attended by thirty-two knights, all his fee'd men, and mostly Yorkshire landowners. If, as wardens, Percies and Nevilles had no authority in Yorkshire, they had plenty as the greatest magnates in the shire.

But, so far as Yorkshire was concerned, the powers of a Percy or a Neville rested on another foundation. The wardens from the early fifteenth century were given a second commission, a rather special commission of the Peace. Henry IV began this practice in 1405, when such commissions were granted to John of Lancaster and Ralph Neville, Earl of Westmorland, and Warden of the West March. Both are specifically called Justice of the Peace *es parties del North*. Dr Rachel Reid has summarized the position in a phrase which cannot be bettered: 'The wardenship of the Marches might be a necessary adjunct to the government of the north, the sign and seal of the authority of the governor; but the basis of that authority was the commission of the peace, whilst the source of the governor's power to enforce it was the vast estates with which the king had enfeoffed him.' The commissions thus granted to Lancaster and Neville differed in extent rather than nature from the ordinary commissions which made justices of the peace of many a small landowner. Whereas the latter served merely for his own county, Lancaster and Neville served for the four northern counties and the three Ridings of Yorkshire. Not only that, but the majority of their fellow justices were their followers and fee'd men.

It is at this point that we must turn back to look at Aske's second point, 'no execution of His Grace's laws'. It is well known that the mark of the period 1377 to 1485 was the 'failure of good governance'. Was the north any worse than other parts of England? Here it is necessary to draw certain distinctions. Most historians have been content to treat the 'parts beyond Trent' as a unity. Although for some administrative purposes they were, we must be prepared to differentiate between Yorkshire and the northern counties. The Vale of York and the East Riding were socially far more closely akin to the midlands, of which they are a geographical extension, than they were to the wild dales of Northumberland, or even the valleys of the West Riding. Unlike the men of Redesdale or Hexham, the Yorkshiremen did not stand in daily, or rather nightly, peril of Scots raids. If a Scots force crossed the Tees it was an invasion, not a mere raid. There was no need for the villagers of the thickly clustered villages of the Vale and the East Riding to sleep with arms ready to hand. The Fitz Hughs might build a towered gate house at Tanfield, or the Metcalfs, a notoriously turbulent family, a pele at Nappa, higher up Wensleydale, but it was more with an eye to local feuds than Scots raids. The Scropes at Bolton in Wensleydale, the Nevilles at Sheriff Hutton, the Percies at Wressle, the Roos at Helmsley, were all building in the late fourteenth century with an eye to comfort rather than defence.

This is not to say that the proximity of the Scots had no effect on Yorkshire. It was the base for really serious operations to the northward. Towns such as York and Beverley were called upon to provide mounted archers or hobelers far more often than southern towns. The subsidies paid by Yorkshire were supposed to be earmarked for the defence of the northern frontier, and there must have been many Yorkshire landowners who made the same sort of agreement with their tenants as did Edward Mauleverer in 1482 with the tenants of his obscure manor of Daletown in Hawnby. Each tenant was to have suitable armour, bow, arrows, sword, shield and horse with doublet and helmet, to serve the king when the lord should call upon him, and failure to obey the summons entailed the forfeiture of the holding. But the tenants of Hawnby did not often ride against the Scots. Obviously local squires who could command such bodies of tenants might be formidable, especially when they felt a deeper loyalty to a local magnate than they did to a distant king. 'Thousands for a Percy!' was no empty war-cry. The north remained feudal longer than the south. It had to, because it was a frontier province. But we must be prepared to draw a distinction between the front line, the real border-country of the East, the West and the Middle March, and the base which was Yorkshire.

The picture of fifteenth-century Norfolk given in the Paston Letters is much the same as that of contemporary Yorkshire in the Plumpton Correspondence. It would be difficult to say which county was the more lawless. Lacking a firm government, the judicial system had virtually broken down. Judges could only act on presentments by juries and juries refused to present. Private prosecutors were trepanned or intimidated. Even if a man were indicted, there was a distinct probability, if he were a man of 'haveage and well friended', that the jury would refuse to convict, in the teeth of the evidence. In the four northern counties assizes were never held more than once a year. Liberties and sanctuaries made the work of the sheriff and his officers extremely difficult. Even as late as the end of Elizabeth's reign the pursuivants of the Council of the North itself were stoned out of the former liberty of Whitby Strand and threatened with death if they laid a hand on one of Cholmley's tenants.

Faced with this situation men turned to other tribunals than the king's judges for settlement of their disputes. For criminal cases the Justices of the Peace could act. It is true that the justices were themselves often law breakers, and on occasion the sessions of the peace ended abruptly with brawling on the bench itself, but they had certain advantages over the judges. They had their Quarter Sessions four times a year, they could act without a formal presentment, they could bind actual or potential evil-doers to the peace, and, above all, where they were local magnates of standing, they had sufficient local power to enforce their decisions.

The Commission of the Peace, on the other hand, was limited to breaches of the peace and breaches of statutes, for example, the Statue of Labourers. It conferred no authority to decide civil actions between party and party. From time to time commissions of oyer and terminer were issued to selected Justices of the Peace, but these were only temporary. So men had recourse more and more frequently to the local and feudal courts to settle their civil actions. Cases were heard by the courts of liberties and honours, and even of baronies and manors. The north becomes a complex patchwork of jurisdictions ranging from great and professional courts like the Chancery Courts of the Bishopric of Durham down to small manorial or baronial courts. As more and more of these smaller courts passed into the hands of the great magnates, their procedure became more professionalized and their decisions were readily enforced. The stewards who held manor courts for the Percies or the Cliffords were highly trained lawyers, sometimes even serjeants-at-law. Behind the steward stood the lord's council ready to enforce the steward's ruling, or to hear and settle disputes between tenants of different manors, or men who were too powerful to be dealt with in the manor courts.

Sir William Plumpton was an important man in the north, Seneschal and Master Forester of the Honour of Knaresborough and Constable of the Castle of Knaresborough. And yet we find him a suitor to the council of the Earl of Northumberland in his suit against Sir William Gascoigne: and when he has a quarrel with Robert Birnand, Northumberland writes telling him not to move in the matter until he has heard the case.

There was, of course, one major restriction on this use of local feudal courts, the old rule that no man might lose his freehold without the king's writ. But even this limitation was more apparent than real, since most of the land in the north was held by customary tenure, copyhold, or lease. Nor was there anything to prevent a dispute involving freehold being referred to the council of a magnate for arbitration if both parties agreed. Hence, by the fifteenth century, the councils of the great northern magnates had become important factors in government. They advised their lord on the management of his household and estates. They advised him in his inevitable lawsuits and disputes. Not infrequently some of the members are retained 'of the council' of York, Hull or other boroughs, and act as agents for their lord in his dealings with the borough. Often it is these men who sit in Parliament for the borough at the costs of their lord. They may do the former good service, but their real interests are pledged to the latter. And, above all, like the King's Council, they are concerned with settling disputes between those who owe allegiance to their lord. It is in the councils of the great magnates, culminating in the council of the Duke of Gloucester, later Richard III, that we can see the germ of the Council of the North.

If the Lancastrians and Yorkists commissioned the Nevilles, Percies, Cliffords, Dacres and other great magnates to govern the country, they, in their turn, depended on the lawyers and lesser landowners who served on their councils. We can see them moving the king to put their councillors on the Commission of the Peace, getting them placed as recorders of the local boroughs or as minor public officials, under-sheriffs or foresters, seneschals or bailiffs of small royal estates, or constables of castles and clerks of markets and the like. Nor was this all; the magnates had patronage of their own. They had estates which needed stewards, castles which needed constables. Offices such as the Wardenship of the Marches gave the right to appoint deputies and constables of castles. There was no lack of pushing and ambitious recruits for these places. The north was bitterly poor, and the service of the greater magnates offered the best chance of a good living to many of the smaller landowners. There were few towns in this part of the country, a bare half dozen that counted; York, Hull, Durham, Newcastle, and Carlisle were the only sizeable ones, and of these only York ranked, by contemporary standards, as a reasonably large town. Hence, as Aske said, there was little trade and few merchants. It was this, more, perhaps, than any other factor, which made the Tudors treat the north as a special area. In the south they could play off the merchant and the smaller landowner against the great magnate. In the north there were few merchants, and the lesser landowner by tradition and habit identified his interests with those of the great local families. Indeed, the same is true of the merchants. We have the witness of the York House Books and the Hull Bench Books for the servile deference paid by those towns to the Earls of Northumberland, and the Percies played a considerable part in the politics of Beverley. Not until the Pilgrimage of Grace disrupted the social structure of the north was it possible for the Tudors even to begin to find the right instruments for the control of the north.

This, however, is to anticipate. The Wars of the Roses found the situation in the north as we have described it; a land in which the king's writ counted for little unless it was backed by the powerful local magnate, where men turned more readily to the lord's council than the king's courts. It was a land, too, where the blood feud still flourished. Fortunately, it is no part of our subject to trace the ramifications of these feuds, but the historian cannot afford to ignore them. And in this respect Yorkshire was no whit behind the other northern counties. To the northerner, at any rate, the Wars of the Roses had a meaning. It was a flare-up of the old feud of Percy and Neville, with other local families of the first and second rank, Cliffords and Dacres, Constables and Eures, throwing in their lot, on one side or the other, in accordance with ancient loyalties or with a shrewd calculation of family interests. The result was that the House of York fell into the role of *tertium gaudens*. Towton broke the power of the Percies, although the attainder was reversed in 1472. Barnet broke the Nevilles, and the bulk of the lands of the Kingmaker were divided between Clarence, who had married one of his daughters, and Gloucester, who was in due season to marry another, the widow of the ill-fated Edward, Prince of Wales.

On the death of Clarence, Gloucester acquired more of the Neville estates, notably Castle Barnard, though the bulk of Clarence's lands reverted to the Crown. Thanks to the Neville inheritance and the virtual monopoly of Crown appointments in the north which Edward IV conferred upon him, Gloucester, from 1472 onwards, was the most powerful man in the north. Though willing to restore the Percies as a counterpoise to the Nevilles, Edward IV had no intention of allowing them to have that predominance which the Nevilles had enjoyed during the first ten years of his reign. Thus though the Earl of Northumberland was pre-eminent in the East Riding and Northumberland, Gloucester, from his castles of Middleham and Sheriff Hutton, ruled Cumberland,

Westmorland and the rest of Yorkshire. His offices ranged from
Warden and Justice of the Forests north of Trent, and High
Steward of the Duchy of Lancaster, down to such minor offices
as the constableship of Scarborough Castle. In 1482 on the
eve of a Scots war he became sole king's lieutenant in
the north. Gloucester and his council were the real rulers of the
north, except for those parts where the authority of Northumberland and his council were more direct. The two magnates
had come to an agreement in 1473 not to recruit each other's
councillors or fee'd men.

Thus, when he came to the throne in 1483, Richard III
had ten or a dozen years' experience of the government of the
north behind him. He knew the country and its problems as no
previous monarch had done. His council at Middleham or
Sheriff Hutton had become a veritable Court of Requests for
the north. The commission of oyer and terminer on which most
of its members sat enabled them, in the king's name, to do
justice between party and party. In particular there is reason
to assume that they enforced the rule that a customary tenant
who performed his services had an action against his lord. It
is certain that they intervened to settle disputes in York and
Hull.

The accession of Richard might have made little difference,
for he seems to have left his council at Sheriff Hutton to serve
for the infant Prince of Wales. But the prince died shortly after
his father's accession, and the whole question was reopened.
Richard determined on a reorganization of the government of
the north. There were two factors to be considered. Northumberland had helped Richard to gain the throne and deserved
his reward. Richard had an instrument to hand for the government of the area in his old council, but in the fifteenth century
such a body needed a figurehead. Northumberland possibly
hoped to step into the position Gloucester had occupied. But
Richard had other ideas. He had realized that the old idea of
including Yorkshire in the Marches, and dividing the March,
broadly speaking, into an eastern and western zone, had little

to commend it. He therefore decided to separate Yorkshire from the March and to reward Northumberland by restoring the family estates in Cumberland and by making him Warden-General of the Marches, constable of all the royal castles in Northumberland and sheriff of that county for life. This, together with numerous minor offices, made Northumberland all-powerful on the Border, for the West March, which was retained by Lord Dacre, was a comparatively small area round Carlisle. Yorkshire was placed under the government of the Earl of Lincoln and a council. Lincoln, though heir to the throne, had no estates in the north, although he was presumably made constable of Sandal Castle where the council sat. It was now obvious that the council would be the king's council and its head the king's lieutenant. The revenues of certain of the royal lands in the north were assigned for its upkeep. North-umberland, it is true, was not entirely excluded; he was a member of the council and his possession of the Honour of Lecon-field and the castles of Wressle and Leconfield gave him con-siderable authority in the East Riding. Hull seems to have regarded him with great deference, though York treated him, on one occasion at least, with some discourtesy. He may have resented his treatment, in fact he probably did, for the Percies seem to have been more attracted to Yorkshire than North-umberland at this period, and his inglorious share in the Bos-worth campaign can only be explained by pique.

Not only did Richard reorganize the government of the north, but the instructions to Lincoln and his council laid down the main lines on which the future Council of the North was destined to develop. The Council was to meet, wholly if possible, at York once every quarter (and oftener if required) to 'order and examine' all bills of complaint. The quorum was fixed to include Lincoln and two councillors. The council was to have power to deal with 'riots, forcible entries, distress tak-ings and other misbehaviours, against our laws and peace'. It was not to try any matter of land without the assent of the parties, a sop to the common lawyers of very little value, for its jurisdiction in matters of distress gave it the right to hear actions of replevin which inevitably involved title to land. Offenders were to be lodged in one of the royal castles 'for we wille that our castles be our gaoles'. All mandates issuing from the Council were to be headed with the words 'By the King' and endorsed at the foot 'And by his Council'. This diplomatic formula lasted till the very end of the Council. There are letters amongst the Hull and York archives as late as 1640 thus endorsed.

Letters involved having a secretary, and the instructions say that one is to be appointed, and that a special seal is to be made for the use of the council. We have no examples of this early seal. The later seal of the Council bore the arms of England, surmounted by a crown and flanked on either side by a hand holding a sword upright.

The instructions made it clear that, in effect, Lincoln's council had criminal jurisdiction, derived from a commission of the peace, and civil, derived from a commission which the instructions say is to be issued and which, presumably, was one of oyer and terminer. Here again, we can see the council of 1484 as the real forerunner of the later Council of the North, whose jurisdiction, right to the very end of its existence, was based on these two commissions. The question may well be asked how the commission of the peace, thus issued, differed from the commissions issued elsewhere. The answer is that it was the same commission, with additions. The obvious intention was that ordinary administrative and routine work was to be left to the landowners and burgesses who sat as Justices of the Peace for the three Ridings and the towns, but that more serious matters were to be handled by the magnates and skilled lawyers who composed the council at Sandal.

With Lincoln's commission the real story of the Council of the North begins. Its history falls into three fairly well defined phases: a period of experiment from 1484 to 1537, the great age of the Council from Henry VIII's commission in 1537 to the end of Lord Burghley's presidency in 1603, and the decline of the Council from 1603 till its virtual suppression by the Long Parliament in 1641.

During the period between the accession of Henry VII and 1537, the history of the Council was by no means continuous. Henry VII looked upon the north with some suspicion. He had to give Northumberland authority there, but was probably by no means sorry when he was killed in a riot. It is probable, but by no means certain, that Henry's mother, the Countess of Richmond, and her council fell into the position occupied by Lincoln under Richard III, and it may well be, as the Plumpton Correspondence seems to indicate, that, towards the end of Henry's reign, the notorious Empson had some special authority in the north. If this be so, it may well account for the fact that, for the first ten years of his reign, Henry VIII seems to have made no effort to establish any sort of special council for the northern counties, other than the wardenships of the East, West, and Middle Marches.

The unpopularity of Empson may have been the reason; another possible explanation is the fact that Wolsey was both Archbishop of York and Bishop of Durham. We are, as yet, somewhat in the dark as to Wolsey's activities in these capacities. His biographers have concentrated on Wolsey as statesman and diplomat, and it has generally been assumed that, because he never visited his northern sees till the end of his career, he was totally uninterested in them. It may be so, but it seems difficult to see why Wolsey, who was notoriously greedy and extravagant, should have been completely uninterested in the Archbishopric and the Bishopric, which between them must have accounted for a goodly proportion of his income, or how, even granting the efficiency of his officials, two such complex structures could have been run without some direction from their lord.

Whatever the reason, the fact is that in the early years of his reign, Henry neither governed the north himself nor found anyone to do it for him. Thus, when the younger Surrey became Lieutenant-General for the Scots war in 1522, he found things in a sorry plight. Dacre, the Warden of the Marches, was frankly incompetent as an administrator. Murder, loot, and rapine were unchecked in the border counties, and the feuds of the Yorkshire gentry, as the Star Chamber records abundantly prove, frequently set whole districts by the ears. The commons were seething with discontent. Enclosure riots were frequent, for the landowners of the north were beginning to feel the pinch of inflation. Customary tenants found that the gressom demanded on a change of tenant, instead of being the traditional amount of twice the rent, was pushed up to six or even ten times. If, unable to meet this demand, the tenant agreed to become a leaseholder, he merely put off the evil day, for the fine for the renewal of a lease was apt to be crippling. The weavers of the West Riding had their own grievances against the clothiers. There is some evidence that the government tried to meet the situation by the standard Tudor method of action by the Council. Quite a number of Star Chamber cases concern the grievances of poor and obscure persons. But petitions to the Star Chamber were sometimes made in order to prevent a poor defendant from making use of one of the local courts, and put him to the expense and inconvenience of a journey to London, though it is only fair to say that the Star Chamber frequently appointed local commissions to hear the case and report. It was this state of affairs which decided Henry and Wolsey to revert to the old idea of a special council for the north.

Henry's illegitimate son, the Duke of Richmond, was to be made Lieutenant, and was to have a Council on the model of Gloucester's. This gave Wolsey an excellent opportunity to place many of his followers, and he seems to have packed the Council very thoroughly. None of its members was above the rank of knight, and ten of its seventeen members were lawyers, five of them canonists, like Higden the Dean of York. Of the five common lawyers, two at least were accustomed to Chancery practice. It is obvious, both from its composition and from such stray references as we have to its working, that it was intended as a Court of Requests for the north. As before, its formal basis was a special commission of the peace and one of oyer and terminer which allowed it to hear cases of treason.*

For a time its authority extended to include the Marches, except the Bishopric of Durham; but, as usual, this did not work, in spite of various sessions held at Newcastle and Carlisle. It needed men of different calibre from Wolsey's lawyers to rule the March, and in 1527 Northumberland was made Warden of the East and Middle Marches, and, a little later, Dacre of the West March, but certain members of Richmond's Council were seconded from Sheriff Hutton to help them. But, in effect, once again Yorkshire was separated from the northern counties. The Council was active, of that there is no doubt. It began by making the local gentry enter into recognizances, whether accused of any offence or not; it seems to have dealt sternly with breaches of the peace and of various statutes. The landowners accused it of slackness in punishing breaches of the statutes against usury and fraudulent clothmaking, but the fact that it seems to have been equally unpopular with the landowners and with the West Riding clothiers indicates that it was active in various directions. Its equity jurisdiction seems to have been popular, for the rebels in 1536 asked that men should not be cited to Westminster, but only to York. This underlines one weakness of Richmond's Council, that litigants with a bad case were inclined to go behind its back to the Star Chamber. For example, Sir Arthur Darcy and Robert Challoner bought some standing timber in Balne, but when their men went to fell it they were driven away by a riotous crowd procured by Anne Neville. Darcy appealed to Richmond's Council which decided in his favour, but Anne refused to accept judgement so that Darcy had to apply for a subpoena to compel appearance before the Privy Council.†

* The commission of the peace is printed in Reid, appendix IV. This is the commission of 1530, but it seems certain that it repeats the earlier commission.

† *Yorkshire Star Chamber Proceedings*, vol. I (Yorkshire Archaeological Society Record Series, vol. XLI), p. 90.

On the fall of Wolsey the gentry, under the leadership of
Lord Darcy, made a determined effort to get rid of the Council.
A long list of grievances was drawn up, especial stress being
naturally laid on the close connection of the Council with
Wolsey, and on the fact that the majority of the councillors were
'spiritual men, not meet to govern us nor other temporal men
in any shire within this your realm'. Henry, however, refused to
rise. He did make certain changes. Richmond's Council became
exclusively his household council, a function it had formerly
exercised along with its wider duties, and a new commission was
issued in 1530 making Tunstall, Bishop of Durham, head of
the new Council. He seems to have been popularly known at
once as 'President of the Council in the North Parts' for there
was a distinction between the commission as king's lieutenant
and that of president. Several members of Richmond's Council
continued to serve on both that and the new Council, but such
new members as Sir Robert Constable of Flamborough had no
connection with Richmond. Tunstall, though he came of a good
Yorkshire family, proved unable to keep order. This infuriated
Henry, who held that his commission should endow the meanest
man with authority. For the moment he was driven back to the
old expedient and in 1532 the Earl of Northumberland was
made Lieutenant.

But Henry (or Cromwell) had decided that the real obstacle
to good governance was the private liberties of the north.
Therefore, from 1533 onwards, he launched an attack on these
liberties. There is no need to go into details here. An enquiry in
1535 showed that the liberties, though still numerous, were not
likely to give much trouble. Many were already in the King's
hands; many of the others were ecclesiastical. Many of these
were suppressed along with the monasteries and two acts, one
for the resumption of liberties and another virtually abolishing
the great sanctuaries, completed the work.* The franchises of
the Archbishop and the Bishop of Durham were spared for the

* The act for the resumption of liberties is printed in G. R. Elton,
Tudor Constitution, Cambridge, 1960, pp. 37 ff.

moment, but fell before long, the former in 1544 on the appointment of Holgate, the latter, though only temporarily, in the reign of Edward VI, to be restored by Mary. The only great lay franchises were those of the Percies and the Dacres. The Dacres, of no great account themselves, had the barony of Greystoke by marriage, and Henry's frontal attack on this failed, when, surprisingly enough, the Lords failed to bring in a verdict of guilty when Henry accused Lord Dacre of treason in 1534. This method could hardly be employed, even by Henry, against the inoffensive Earl of Northumberland, so a more indirect method was tried. Henry bought up the numerous debts which the unfortunate Earl had inherited from his predecessor, Henry the Magnificent, and had increased himself, and put the screw on him. After much intrigue he agreed to disinherit his brother, who was his heir, and to surrender his lands to Henry in return for an annuity of £1,000 per annum. The year which saw the suppression of the monasteries also saw the Percy lands fall into the King's hands. A similar method was applied to a less important, but still powerful magnate, Sir Francis Bigod of Settrington and Mulgrave.

Such were the conditions in 1536 when the varied and complicated grievances of the north flared up in the Pilgrimage of Grace. It would be too much to say that it was caused by Henry's attack on the liberties, but this was undoubtedly one of the main causes. The part played by the Council in the Pilgrimage was peculiar. Northumberland was a sick man and could take no active part, and the lead seems to have been taken by Lord Darcy as constable of Pontefract. After putting up a token resistance, the Council went over to the rebels, and put their demands to Henry. What is more interesting from the present point of view is the use made by Henry of the Council. In December 1536, Norfolk replaced Northumberland as Lieutenant and a new Council was formed which contained many of the former members. These were the chosen instruments of Henry's vengeance, and such men as Sir William Eure, Sir Ralph Ellerker and Robert Bowes are commissioned to take the indictments of the rebels, including their relatives and fellow councillors, Sir Robert Constable, Darcy, Aske, and Sir Thomas Percy. Never was the maxim *divide et impera* more cynically or successfully employed. The failure of the rebellion had driven a wedge between gentry and commons, and its suppression split the gentry into irreconcilable factions. Henceforward men like Bowes and Ralph Ellerker could only look to the king for help and support. To their fellows they must have appeared as double dyed traitors. Henry now had the men to make the Council of the North a potent force, whilst the attainder of several of the greatest abbots for complicity in the Pilgrimage and the speedy surrender of the others increased both Henry's actual power and his capacity to reward good service.

The Council established in 1537 was destined to be no mere temporary expedient, but to become a permanent feature of the Tudor and early Stuart system of government. Within the year, we find Norfolk writing to Henry to say that the north was reduced to order and there was no further need of a lieutenant, it could quite well be ruled by a president and council, and from the appointment of Tunstall as Lord President in 1537 there is an unbroken sequence of lords president except from 1596 to 1599 when Archbishop Hutton filled the office, but was not commissioned.

In a more detailed study of the Council it would be necessary to trace the alterations in the instructions given to the various lords president. But as these were not of outstanding importance, it may suffice to sketch in broad outline the structure and functions of the Council as established by Henry and modified by himself and his successors. In the first place we must note one important difference between the Council and most of its predecessors. It was purely judicial and governmental and had, unlike such councils as Gloucester's or Richmond's, no responsibility for the financial administration of estates, royal or baronial. Up to 1600 many of the councillors, except the lawyers, held royal offices, such as stewardships of manors, or wardenships of liberties, but the Council as a body had no responsibility for the administration of Crown lands.

The extent of its jurisdiction was all England north of the Humber, except the Palatinate of Lancaster. It was to hold its quarterly sessions in York, Newcastle, Durham, and Hull, but, as usual, it soon became apparent that the Borders could not be controlled except, as Norfolk told Henry, by 'men of good estimation and nobility'. Therefore after 1541, when Norfolk went north as Lieutenant-general, the old system was renewed. In time of war the commander of the army and, in time of peace, the wardens controlled the Borders, communicating directly with the Privy Council on all Border questions, though orders relating to civil administration were sent through the Lord President for transmission to the justices of the peace. But although it lost direct control of the Borders, the Council continued to entertain civil actions and hold discretionary sessions from time to time in Carlisle and Newcastle.

The Council consisted of a president and a varying number of councillors. Usually there were three of four lords, half a dozen knights and about the same number of lawyers, some of them common lawyers and some civilians or canonists. The number of councillors fluctuates but tends to increase. Under Elizabeth, for example, the Archbishop of York, the Bishop of Durham and the Deans of both cathedrals were invariably included. Under Henry and Edward VI the laymen almost without exception were royal officials, escheators, stewards, and so forth, but later it became the custom to include one or more of the leading landowners of each of the Ridings. The councillors were, of course, compelled to take an oath, not dissimilar from that of a privy councillor. The ideals which Henry set before the Council were 'the quietness and good governance of the people' and 'speedy and indifferent administration of justice between party and party.' To this we may add the enforcement of Henry's changes in religion and other reforms. The commissions were the old two, the Peace, and Oyer and Terminer, amplified by the instructions now given to each Lord President.

The Council was to hold four general sessions a year, each lasting a month. These sessions dealt with civil business first, and criminal after the civil cases had been heard. Whilst it could, and did, use the common law procedure of indictment and verdict, it could also use, as it more frequently did, the Star Chamber method of bill, witness, and examination. In fact the common law process was restricted to treason, murder, and felony. The other method, allowing as it did the examination of the defendant and the compulsion of witnesses to give evidence, was obviously more satisfactory. It had the further advantage that it could be applied to cases between party and party. At its speediest, an action before the Council began by the sub-mission of a bill by the plaintiff to which the defendant had to reply. Then the parties, having taken the ex-officio oath, were examined on interrogatories, the evidence of witnesses was taken either on affidavit before one of the examiners of the court, or by depositions before commissioners. A day was then set for hearing when counsel on both sides were heard and the decree of the Council was given. Of course, the proceedings might be protracted, but generally speaking it seems to have worked expeditiously. Any attempt to bring vexatious complaints was checked by the award of heavy damages against the plaintiff. Process was cheap, as the fees were fixed and the attorneys were officers of the court which could, and presumably did, tax their costs. Much, of course, depended on the Lord President. Under a solid, conscientious worker like Huntingdon (1572–95) the Council worked efficiently and smoothly, but under a venal or lazy ruler like Archbishop Young (1561–8) or Sheffield (1603–19) things went badly and the Council became un-popular.

Before considering the officers of the Council it should be noted that, amongst the councillors, a distinction is drawn, especially from 1568 onwards, between ordinary councillors and those who are 'bound to continual attendance.' These were the common lawyers who had board and lodging in the president's house, each with three or four servants according to rank, and

a fee of £50 for an esquire or £66 13s. 4d. for a knight, raised
in 1579 to a uniform £100. There were always at least four of
these councillors who formed the quorum. One, at least, with
the president had to be present at every session. The president
and some of these councillors were after 1550 sworn as masters
in chancery, so that they could take recognizances. As time
went on the other councillors tended to leave the legal business
to professionals, and usually only attended at the beginning of
the general sessions to hear the reading of the commission. In
Elizabeth's reign a rota of the legal members was established,
one of whom was continually in residence at York to deal with
urgent business.

Next to the president came the vice-president who acted in
the former's absence. He provided what might be called the
permanent element. Sir Thomas Gargrave, who held the office
under five presidents and served the Council thirty-four years
(1545–79) was perhaps the most powerful man in the north. He
was the last lawyer to hold the office, a fact of some importance,
since it meant that henceforth there was always a non-lawyer
on the Council, and though the president lost his veto when the
Council sat as a law court, he had a vote which was decisive if
the legal members were equally divided. The fact that neither
president nor vice-president was a lawyer saved the Council
from becoming too professionalized.

The next member was the secretary with a fee of 50 marks.
But the perquisites were numerous, as the secretary was keeper
of the signet and had fees for sealing. From 1556 onwards the
Council had an attorney, an extremely important official
inasmuch as his duty was to 'prosecute ... for Her Majesty as
well by way of Information as Indictment, all offences of Treason, Murder, Felony, etc.' This meant that the Council was in
no way tied to the procedure by jury of presentment. The
attorney could prosecute on mere information which, considering the imperfections of Tudor juries, must have put a strong
weapon in the hands of the Council. The attorney, unlike the
secretary, was not sworn of the Council. He was a mere officer

of the court, concerned with its legal business only. All fines and amercements passed through his hands.

Below him came two examiners of witnesses, appointed by the president and Council, and the registrar, appointed by the secretary, who kept a register of attachments, list of recognizances and cases pending. Other officials of the secretary's office were two clerks of the seal, drawing £100 per annum, a clerk of the tickets who copied answers to bills and evidence taken on commission. There were also fourteen clerks who also acted as attorneys. They were paid the fees for king's letters and bills, about £600 per annum, and 2s., later raised to 2s. 6d., per sitting when acting as attorneys. As the sheriff was the subordinate of the Council and had to make attachments and serve processes on its orders, he found it essential to have a deputy in attendance, and appointed a clerk of attachments, usually the president's private secretary. The Council did not rely exclusively on the sheriff for executions but had a pursuivant, and later a serjeant at arms, with ten collectors of fines and two tipstaves. In most serious matters it seems to have preferred to trust its own staff to make arrests, particularly of recusants, leaving only the more formal business to the sheriff and his staff. The total membership of the Council, then, was about thirty, but if we add servants, grooms, personal secretaries, and the inevitable hangers-on of a great Elizabethan establishment, we can probably reckon that there were not far short of 100 people in and about the Council.

To move a body of this size, with its registers, rolls, and other paraphernalia was no easy matter. Hence the Council tended to fix itself more and more at York. At first, as we have seen, it had to hold sessions at York, Newcastle, Hull, and Durham. By 1556 Hull drops out, and Carlisle replaces Durham, to drop out or share a session with Newcastle from 1561; and by 1582 the president was left complete discretion as to where sessions were held, which, in practice, meant that they were always held at York. The suggestion in 1597 that a session at

Newcastle might be necessary seems to have caused considerable consternation to the local authorities.

The housing of the court became a problem when Holgate,
then Bishop of Llandaff, became president in 1538. Unlike his
predecessors, he had no castle or residence near York, and we
find the Council asking for a grant of the Blackfriars on Toft
Green. A better solution was found by giving it the abbot's
lodging and site of the Abbey of St Mary, suppressed in 1540.
Not only was this more commodious, but it lay just outside the
walls of the city and had always been exempt from the jurisdiction of the civic authorities. Abbot Sever had recently (about
1490–1500) rebuilt part of it, but it soon became too small for
the needs of the Council, and most of the presidents, from
Shrewsbury to Strafford, added to it. The building with its
magnificient doorways, fireplaces and ceilings still testifies to the
might and authority of the Council of the North.* It also
acquired the King's Manor (formerly the Austin Friars) at
Newcastle, which as the Newcastle sessions were reduced and
abandoned gradually degenerated into a mere store-house.

The Council was no mere dependency of the Privy Council.
North of the Humber it exercised the administrative and
judicial functions of the Council. After the foundation of the
High Commission in 1559 some of its duties in the enforcement of the religious settlement were taken over by the latter,
but the two bodies worked in harmony and there was considerable duplication of membership.

As a court the Council dealt with both criminal and civil
matters. Its criminal work ties up closely with its administrative
duties, but its civil work was of the utmost importance. Coke
said in 1607 that it dealt with 2,000 cases a year. This was
probably an exaggeration, for Coke was making out a case
against the Council. But it is a fact that any collection of
private muniments in the north which covers the period 1540–
1640 is almost certain to yield several cases heard before the

---

* The building now houses part of the University of York. It has been
described by Davis, *History of the King's Manor*, York, 1883.

Council. Theoretically, it could not touch freehold, but it frequently did, either by consent of the parties or by replevin. The archives of York and Hull indicate that it entertained cases in which citizens or burgesses were concerned. Hull Trinity House, in drafting the conditions of appointment of its secretary in 1591, thought it sufficiently important to lay down that the secretary must ride to York when necessary at his own cost, and the records show that these journeys to York were often about cases before the Council.

The bulk of the civil cases were actions relating to ejection, tenant right, leasehold, and debt. At the one end of the scale, we see it dealing with important problems like the title to the great Dacre estates; at the other, with small debts of a few pounds. Its decision that the normal fine for renewal of a lease should not be more than twice the rent served as a precedent for the later custom enforced by the courts of Westminster.

Ellesmere, as Lord Chancellor, made it a rule to refer cases in equity to the Council when both parties were resident in the north. If either party claimed to be too poor to sue his case at Westminster, the Council had jurisdiction. This led to some trouble as it was impossible to say whether a man was, in fact, too poor to respond. A more sensible rule was the one that came to be applied in cases of non-payment of rent for lease-hold, where the Council had jurisdiction if the amount in dispute was less than £40. Of the convenience and popularity of the civil jurisdiction of the Council there can be no doubt. The frequent petitions under the Commonwealth and in the early years of Charles II for some sort of Court of Requests at York, and the almost invariable clause in eighteenth-century York-shire conveyances, restricting the liability of parties to a fine not to travel beyond York, are proofs of the fact that the court met a genuine need.

It is extremely difficult to differentiate between the criminal and administrative duties of the Council. Formally, of course, the criminal business was the suppression of offences like murder, robbery, and arson, which were felonies at common law, whilst the administrative business was the enforcement of statutes, for example, those against seminary priests. But the effect and the machinery were much the same in both cases, and the authority derived from one or other of its commissions.

Under pressure from the government the Council tended to emphasize now one, now another, of its administrative duties, but it was fairly consistent in one, the general supervision of the justices of the peace. We are so accustomed to think of the justices as the 'maids of all work of the Tudor government', that we are apt to forget what very unsatisfactory servants they were. The stupid justice is a common figure in eighteenth- and nineteenth-century literature, and no one imagines that the mere insertion of a squire's name in the commission of the peace made him any wiser or more judicial. But, on the whole, the eighteenth- or early nineteenth-century justice was a willing agent of government policy, administering, in the county, the laws which he and his fellows had made at Westminster. But the Tudor justice was not only, very often, stupid: he was frequently venal, quarrelsome and disloyal. Statutes which suited his own interests he would enforce, and cheerfully ignore those which did not. It would have been fatuous to expect a rigorous enforcement of the recusancy laws in the North Riding, or the laws regulating the cloth trade in the West Riding. Even those justices whose personal interests were not involved would not make themselves unpopular by excess of zeal. This was not a peculiarity of the northern justices; it was common to the whole country, but, whereas the justices of the home counties and the midlands could be kept up to the mark by the combined efforts of the Privy Council and the Lords Lieutenant, those of the north were too far away. Also, it would seem that, in the south, there was no lack of suitable candidates for the commission, while the field was more restricted in the north.

Here we have the explanation of the value and the unpopularity of the Council in its administrative capacity. It had the power and the will to enforce the policy of the government, or, at need, to see that the justices enforced it, whether they wanted to or not. The result was that the Council, in its administrative aspect, enjoyed an unpopularity which it never had as a court of civil jurisdiction, and it was the county gentry, assembled in the Long Parliament, who finally destroyed it.

On the administrative side, the history of the Council falls into four phases which coincide with the reigns of Henry VIII, Edward VI and Mary, Elizabeth, and the early Stuarts. Under Henry the first object of the Council was to reduce the north to order, after the Pilgrimage of Grace. We find it busy punishing riots and breaches of the peace, taking sureties of suspected persons, and active in enforcing Henry's religious settlement. Above all it seems to have been active in making enquiry as to intakes and enclosures, landlords taking excessive gressoms and exorbitant rents, and in giving remedy to the sufferers. The result was that the county was so far pacified that Henry was able to pay a long-deferred visit to York in 1541, and the agrarian troubles of 1547 found no echo in the north. By a judicious combination of firmness and conciliation, the Council had gone far to settle the problem of the north by the time of Henry's death.

Under his son, however, the Council became the sport of factions. Somerset, who had packed the Council with his supporters and who wanted to use it to push his economic and religious policy, naturally gave it full support, and even extended its authority, ordering the mayor and aldermen of York to obey its instructions notwithstanding their charters. But with the fall of Somerset in 1549, Warwick changed all this. He pushed Holgate out and put Shrewsbury in as president, and altered the personnel of the Council, though only slightly. But the fact was that he could not trust a predominantly Catholic body to enforce his religious policy. He feared it might unite with Somerset against him. Therefore he set about increasing his own power in the north. He took over the wardenship of the Marches, made himself high steward of the bishopric of Durham, and reduced the Council of the North to the level, as Dr Rachel Reid puts it, of 'a glorified court of Quarter

Sessions'. Some of the powers the Council then lost it never regained. The Borders passed from its control, its members were never again commissioners of sewers, or for collecting subsidies, also it was never again included as a whole in the ordinary commission of the peace for the northern shires. Shrewsbury, a perfect time-server, who held on to his office till the reign of Elizabeth, was not the man to resist these encroachments. He was frequently absent from the north for long periods, and, when he was there, usually resided at his castle at Sheffield, quite the most inconvenient centre in the whole county. The result was that, even when he was in residence, the councillors bound to continual attendance found it difficult to get their diet and attend to their business, and in his absence the vice-president had neither the funds nor the accommodation to support them. From this slough the Council was pulled by the activity of its new vice-president, Sir Thomas Gargrave, who was appointed in 1555. His plans were furthered by a disquieting report on the state of the Borders. The justices of the peace, too, were in need of a strong hand and the Privy Council bluntly told them that if they failed to amend their ways they would be called to York to answer for their faults. Thus Elizabeth found the Council a much stronger body than it had been three years earlier.

It needed to be, for the claims of Mary Queen of Scots revived the problem of the north. But Elizabeth's religious settlement gave the old problem a new turn. Hitherto, the one constant factor in northern politics had been hatred of the Scots. Henceforward, hostility to Elizabeth's church settlement implied, in strict logic, a readiness to accept the Scots candidate to the throne. Whether Elizabeth weighed this in determining her policy or not, we have no means of knowing. Recent work by Mr Aveling, Dr McGrath, Dr Claire Cross, and others has revealed the extent and complexity of the problem of recusancy in the north. There were plenty of opponents of the new order, but many were pure traditionalists whose opposition would never be active, especially if it implied support of the Scot. In the West Riding there were, as Professor Dickens has shown, a number of advanced Protestants. There was also the possibility of an alternative to Mary in the house of Lennox, until Mary's marriage to Darnley united the claim of both branches of the Stuarts. Under these circumstances Elizabeth at first moved warily. Shrewsbury, in spite of his opposition to the Act of Uniformity, was continued in office till his death in 1560, and the main function of the Council seems to have been to enforce the economic policy of the government. The death of Shrewsbury and the Treaty of Leith opened the way for a more vigorous policy. The revised instructions of 1561 contemplated a drive to enforce the religious policy, and the establishment of a permanent court at York. Rutland as president proposed to restore and extend the King's Manor. The rule that one or more of the legal councillors should always be in residence also strengthened the Council, and the Queen's Attorney received extensive powers to prosecute.

Rutland, however, died in 1563, and was followed in 1564 by Archbishop Young, probably the worst of all the presidents. Vain, stupid, idle, and greedy, one wonders why Elizabeth tolerated him, even for a year. So far from enforcing the religious policy, he let things slide, and even appointed as councillors men like Sir John Constable, who was very untrustworthy in religion. Perhaps for the moment a pliable president suited Elizabeth, for it was during Young's presidency that the government intervened in certain important matters like the Dacre lands, and the enforcement of a rule to compel tenants to enclose lands near the Border with quickset hedges, in both of which matters the decision of the Council was set aside. Young made no attempt to hold the sessions outside York, or to enforce the laws about tillage and armour. He kept no proper books of decrees, allowed members of the Council to appear before it professionally on behalf of parties, and let cases drag on indefinitely. So, at any rate, says a memorial of 1568. One is inclined to suspect exaggeration, for the Council handled the rebellion of the northern earls, in 1569, on the whole very successfully.

But it was probably as well that Young died within a month or two of the flight of Mary into England. The achievement of the Council in 1569 is the more remarkable when we remember its abject failure in 1536, and that Sussex, the new president, had been sent north to carry out quite a different policy from that finally adopted. The Council was kept busy from 1569 to 1570 stamping out the embers of the revolt, trying and fining the gentry and dealing severely with the lesser offenders. Many became vagrants and masterless men, and the Council had to deal severely with them. The hard work fell on Gargrave, the vice-president, for Cecil was only too glad to let Sussex retire, once he had finished with the rebellion, in 1570. In fact he induced his retirement by a series of pinpricks.

With the appointment of Huntingdon as president in 1572, we reach the great age of the Council. Its powers had been built up, as we have seen, by successive commissions and instructions, culminating in 1561, but, hitherto, for political and probably personal reasons, they had never been used to the full. The new president was the Queen's cousin, an ardent Protestant, and entirely without territorial importance in the north. His estates were mostly in the midlands and his authority in the north derived solely from his commission. He was a Puritan and under his rule the north was godly, if not always quietly governed. Generally speaking, he had the backing of the Privy Council, and Cecil worked well with him. As a civil court the Council continued to function smoothly, and, on the whole, beneficently. Huntingdon, though 'raw at first', as his colleague Archbishop Hutton said later, 'became by study and diligence a good President'. He was regular in his attendance to business and put an end to the slackness of Young's regime. We see him giving judgements against landlords who were still trying to take unconscionable gressoms, and not only in Yorkshire. The prebendaries of Durham and Sir Henry Curwen in Cumberland fell under his judgement. He decided the

complaints brought by the workmen against the German mining
adventurers in the Lake District. On the administrative side,
the Council was most active. Its activities fell into three main
categories – defence, the supervision of local authorities, and
the enforcement of the various enactments about recusants,
vagrants, the cloth and corn trades, the poor, and so forth.

Although it has been stated that Huntingdon's duties in the
preparations for defence arose from his commission as Lord
Lieutenant and not from his office as Lord President, it seems
that his contemporaries failed to make this distinction. At any
rate, we find him and the Council busy in taking musters, training the able men, providing drafts for overseas, and seeing
that the coast is watched and the beacons in readiness. He
hears complaints of the activities of the Dunkirkers and asks
the Lord Admiral to grant letters of marque to a Newcastle
barque against them. A Scarborough man who had dealings
with pirates was arrested by the Council, which also sought to
induce the Humber ports to help a local man, who had built a
large privateer, to find the money to equip it.

More important were its dealings with an early ship-money
case. The controversy had begun as far back as 1547, but
became acute in the year of the Armada. Hull had always con-
tended that the outports, which were joined to it for certain
customs purposes, should help it to support the burden of
providing ships for the royal service. In particular it claimed
that York should help. The point had never been properly
settled when, in 1588, Hull was ordered to equip two ships and
pinnaces and victual them for two months. Huntingdon was
ordered to urge the outports, and the towns using Hull as their
port, to contribute. On their refusal, he bound over the local
mayors to appear before the Privy Council. The ports gave in,
but York had to be coerced and judgement was given by the
Privy Council that it should pay £600 towards the £1,015
which the ships had cost. This time it seems that the West
Riding towns escaped, but when the question arose again over
the Cadiz expedition, they were forced to contribute. Though

the ultimate decision here rested with the Privy Council, it acted consistently through the Council of the North.

The ship-money case leads naturally to a discussion of the control exercised by the Council over the local authorities. So far as the towns were concerned the Council intervened in disputes between towns, as, for example, in a dispute between York and Hull over the lead trade. We also find it intervening in internal dispute in towns, as at Newcastle and York, where, on the instructions of the Privy Council, it even arrested the Mayor in 1579. At York, too, it passed on instructions to the Mayor on a variety of matters, calling upon him to fix prices of board and lodging for suitors to the Council, to enforce the laws against regrating and forestalling, to take a census of beggars, and to enforce vagrancy laws. Huntingdon kept an eye on elections, and there is a letter from him to Hull in 1586 asking for the nomination of one member and instructing the Mayor to take care that the other should be 'knowne to be religious and well affected to her Majestie'. The Council similarly kept a strict eye on the county justices, trying to see that they did their numerous duties, and ready either to take order with them or to act itself in their default. For example, a bridge near Sedbergh was destroyed in 1585. This was strictly a matter for the local justices to attend to, but the Council appointed commissioners to get the bridge repaired. When the local justices refused to enforce the act of 1593 against stretching cloth, the Council stepped in and enforced it.

It was the same in other directions, and the Council had to bear a lot of opprobrium for enforcing unpopular acts. When it was dealing with the spreading of false rumours, vagrancy and breaches of the peace, it had popular feeling behind it on the whole, but the enforcement of the religious legislation tended to make it unpopular. In Huntingdon, a precise Puritan, the government had a president who was willing to run the risk. He began hopefully, with the idea that recusancy could be stamped out, but after the seminary priests began to come over he confessed in 1576 that 'the declination in matters of

7—TT * *

religion is very great'. The Blockhouse at Hull, York Castle and other gaols were soon full, many prisoners dying of the infection of the prison. From 1582 to 1592 there were generally one or more executions a year. Perhaps the most famous victim was Margaret Clitheroe, but she actually died under the *peine forte et dure* for refusing to plead. Huntingdon was strict, but not merciless. He refused to exercise the full rigour of the law against harbourers of priests, and seems to have done what he could to mitigate the lot of the numerous gentlewomen imprisoned.

The punishments inflicted by the Council were fines, the pillory, wearing of papers and imprisonment. They were not, by contemporary standards, unduly severe. In fact, on occasion, the Privy Council asked for more severity, as in the case of an impostor claiming to be a sailor despoiled by the Spaniards. The Privy Council told them to nail his ear to the pillory and after, if they saw cause, to lop it off. It may be as well to say that the Council had no power to use torture, and there is no proof that it did so; though there are hints that the Privy Council would not have objected if, on occasion, it had.

Another function of the Council was that of trying to combat the litigiousness of the times. One example will suffice. Two Hull merchants, John Barker and Thomas Mountague, had been taken prisoner by the Dunkirkers, and, though at liberty, dared not return to Hull to face their creditors. The Council called the creditors before it, and sought to compel them to treat the unfortunates leniently.

With the death of Huntingdon, the decline of the Council begins. There were several reasons for this. There was a bitter struggle for the control of the Council between Essex and Cecil, which Cecil ultimately won, but only at the price of packing the Council and giving way to the local gentry. The main reason for this was the increased importance of Scottish affairs in the last decade of Elizabeth's reign. Cecil was backing James, realizing that if Essex and his party had their way and supported Arabella, there was serious risk of a Scottish attack on northern England at a very critical time. Both parties were therefore seeking support from the Yorkshire gentry and towns. It is true that under Hutton as locum tenens, and Burghley as president, the persecution of the recusants was increased. It had not much effect. Whitby and the surrounding country was a safe refuge for seminaries, and when, after elaborate preparations, the Council staged a raid on a notorious 'nest of Papists' at Grosmont, a few miles up the Esk from Whitby, they found that the birds had flown. Whitby had also shown its hostility to the Council by driving out one of the officers of the Council who came to serve a process.

The Council, however, was under fire from various quarters. Thanks to Burghley's lavish creation of new councillors, it was becoming too large for an administrative body, and the government was increasingly corresponding direct with the sheriffs and justices. It still, however, used the Council when speed and secrecy were necessary. Ferne, the secretary, wrote to the Mayor of Hull on 7 November 1605, to inform him of the Gunpowder Plot and instruct him to keep watch for Sir Henry Percy. Ferne adds a post script, 'Haste truly made me take a broken shard of paper'.

As early as 1595 the North Riding justices rebelled against a writ of supersedeas issued in a case pending before them. 'They would either be justices or no justices.' The West Riding justices followed suit. Then Serjeant Yelverton treated the president with gross discourtesy at the Assizes in 1600. A little later Lord Willoughby denied its right to effect an arrest at Berwick. On the whole the government supported the Council. Yelverton was ordered to apologize, the justices were punished, and a way found of making its supersedeas legal. But it was the writing on the wall. If litigants who took their cases to the Council could be imprisoned or compelled to enter bond by the local justices, its value was going to be diminished. When Sheffield became president in 1603, a significant change was made. The legal members were to have precedence over all others below the rank of barons' sons. This emphasized the fact that the legal functions of the Council henceforward took precedence over the administrative.

Even these did not escape attack. Already they had been definitely subordinated to Chancery and it had been decided that the Council could not stay proceedings in the courts of Westminster. But, having gained its victory, Chancery used it with moderation, and it is doubtful if the subordination meant the loss of much business.

Very soon the common law courts moved to the attack under the doughty leadership of Coke. Prohibitions and writs of habeas corpus began to be issued against the Council, and these were signs that it might follow the Court of Requests into oblivion. Coke, who had admitted its jurisdiction when it suited his purpose, quoted much false history and dubious law against it. The only substantial objection was met in 1609, when the instructions, as well as the commission, were enrolled, so that the exact powers of the court were known to all men. The fall of Coke ended the attack for the time, and, despite his decision that the Council was illegal, it functioned for thirty years after his fall. The opposition of the towns became more vocal. In 1607 York raised the problem of the rights of precedence of its mayor and the president but got little by it beyond a tart suggestion from the Privy Council that it should learn to rule its citizens. The attitude of the towns was illogical but understandable. They were ready to use the Council in their disputes or deny its jurisdiction as suited their convenience for the moment. It is therefore impossible to say that they hated or favoured the Council. York opposed it on occasion, but petitioned for its restoration in 1642.

But, although we cannot, owing to the loss of its record, say much with certainty about this phase of its history, a few main trends do appear. In spite of prohibitions, it continued to handle a lot of civil business. There was considerable building and rebuilding of the King's Manor by Sheffield and Strafford, which bears out the suggestion that the Council still had plenty of business. But Sheffield and Scrope were not the sort of presidents to inspire respect. Sheffield, who was not above using his official position to help his private speculations in the alum monopoly, was quite ready to sell any office in the Council, and Scrope was nearly as bad. Sir Arthur Ingram, as his correspondence with Sir Henry Slingsby shows, was entirely concerned with his fees. In fact, the Council suffered from the universal corruption of the times.

The Council, in the event, became something of a storm centre of politics between 1625 and 1628. Sheffield had been dismissed for his too-zealous attacks on the recusants. Scrope therefore took office in 1619 as agent of a more lenient policy, which naturally aroused the hostility of the West Riding Puritans, led by Sir John Savile. Briefly, Savile appears as the leader of the clothing interest whilst Wentworth represented the country gentry whose interests as wool producers were opposed to that of the clothiers. Savile, a shifty character, put up Wentworth to succeed him as *custos rotulorum* in the West Riding, when he was compelled to resign in 1615, expecting that, if he made his peace with the government, Wentworth would resign in his favour. But Wentworth did not, even when asked by Buckingham in 1617. This began a life-long feud, fought out partly in elections from 1621 and partly in the Council to which Wentworth was nominated in 1619. In a brief study it is impossible to follow the details. The key figure was Buckingham, who, it should be remembered, was a Yorkshire landowner of considerable importance thanks to his inheritance of the Roos lands. By supporting Buckingham, Savile became vice-president in 1626 and though Scrope retained the presidency, the real power was in his hands, and he soon acquired the profitable office of Receiver of Recusancy fines, north of Trent. Ingram, who had been dropped from the Council in 1625 for corruption, jumped on the bandwagon and was restored in 1626. The assassination of Buckingham in 1628 completely altered the situation. Wentworth who had been imprisoned for his opposition to the forced loan in 1627 was returned to Parliament for Yorkshire in 1628 and took the lead in the passing of the Petition of Right. His opposition had been to Buckingham's foreign policy, not to Charles, and by now the corruption of the Buckingham faction had become an open scandal. So Savile and Scrope were dismissed in 1628, though Savile was still a member of the Council, and Wentworth was appointed as Lord President. He took office prepared to enforce his policy of 'Thorough'.

He laid down, in his first speech as president, the two principles which he proposed to adopt; not to exceed by a hair's breadth the limits of the commission and instructions, and to refer all prohibitions 'to His Majesty, the sovereign judge of us all'. Despite numerous attacks he held to this policy and the government backed him. The opposition, led now by Lord Fauconberg, tried their best to flout Wentworth and deny the authority of the Council, but Fauconberg was ultimately sent to London to make his submission.

Wentworth was unlucky; he took office as the leader of the party of the country gentry, but he wanted to help the poor man and ensure even-handed government. It was his misfortune that the various expedients for raising money tried by Charles I, distraint of knighthood, revival of the Forest and the rest, fell mainly on the shoulders of the former supporters who soon turned against him. Maleverer, who refused to compound for not taking up knighthood, unless compelled by common law process, got his case tried in the Exchequer in 1631; the court refused to fine him but issued warrants for distress to the amount of £2,000, most of which he had to pay. Sir David Foulis, a member of the Council, annoyed at being dropped from the commission for compounding with recusants, began a series of slanderous attacks on Wentworth, alleging that he had pocketed most of the knighthood fines. Wentworth naturally brought an action for slander, and Foulis and his son were heavily fined by Star Chamber. Both refused to pay and remained in the Fleet for seven years until released by the Long Parliament. In 1633 Sir John Bourchier led a riot and broke the fences of an enclosure the King had made in the Forest of Galtrees. The King remitted the case to the Council which fined Bourchier £1,800. After he had been six months in prison, Wentworth, at the request of the Council, interceded with the King on his behalf. Attempts against the equity jurisdiction of the Council were similarly resisted, and in 1633 a new set of instructions was drafted. Though these were later quoted in the articles of impeachment against Wentworth, they really contained nothing new and the managers of the impeachment did not find them a very good weapon.

When the Long Parliament met, however, there were plenty of opponents of the Council. The common lawyers hated it for professional reasons and Hyde was chairman of a committee of the House which reported strongly against it. The new Yorkshire families, the Saviles, Hothams, Fairfaxes, Vanes, who had replaced the Percies, Eures, Constables, and Ellerkers as the leading men of the county, were all hostile to Wentworth and the Council. After the execution of Wentworth the attack was launched. Though the Commons resolved against the Council, the Lords hesitated. They finally condemned its Star Chamber jurisdiction and, with reservations, its equity jurisdiction. But they coupled with this the recognition of the need for a court at York. All this took time, and though the Grand Remonstrance spoke of it as 'a forge of misery, oppression and violence', Charles could tell the assembled gentry at York in 1642 with truth that 'he knew no legal dissolution of it. It is rather shaken in pieces than dissolved'.

That might well stand for the epitaph of the Council of the North. The York tradesmen who saw in its abolition the loss of profitable customers, the small man who had found it a cheap and speedy tribunal for the collection of debts and the settlement of disputes – these might regret its passing; but the Fairfaxes, the Cholmleys, and the Saviles who had been fined for ship-money, encroachments on forests, or other similar offences could, and did, regard it as an instrument of oppression.

Hence the numerous efforts to restore it failed. The north

and its difficulties were of little interest to the south country gentry and lawyers of Cromwell's Parliaments. After the Restoration grand juries all over the county, in York and Hull, as well as in the three Ridings, petitioned for its restoration, and, for a moment, it looked as though they might succeed. But the Yorkshire Plot of 1662 which made it obvious that any court at York would have to wield administrative authority, and the implacable hostility of its old enemy Hyde, now Lord Chancellor Clarendon, prevented its revival, though there seems to have been some idea of it in 1665 which came to nothing.

It may be that the decision was right. The conciliar system had been weighed in the balance and found wanting. The problems of the north in the age which was dawning in 1660 were not those which Aske had outlined a century before. Those problems had been settled, largely by the work of the Council of the North. And yet there was substance in the petitions for the restoration of the Council. The impact of the industrial changes of the eighteenth century on the north might have been very different had there been at York a court to carry on into the age of the Industrial Revolution the traditions of the civil and equitable jurisdiction of the Council of the North.

BIBLIOGRAPHICAL NOTE

The fundamental, indeed the only, book on the Council of the North is R. R. Reid, *The King's Council in the North* (London, 1921). J. R. Tanner, *Tudor Constitutional Documents* (Cambridge, 1922), prints several documents, including Coke's arguments against the Council, and the Instructions of 1545 with a brief commentary. G. R. Elton, *Tudor Constitution* (Cambridge, 1960) prints the Regulations of 1484 and the Instructions of c. 1544 with a valuable commentary and carries this further in his *Policy and Police* (Cambridge, 1972). A. W. Prothero prints the Commission of 1603 with a commentary in *Select Statutes and other documents* (Oxford, 1906). The relations of the Council with the Borders are considered in T. I. Rae, *Administration of the Scottish Frontier 1513–1603* (Edinburgh, 1967). We know much more than we did a decade ago about the activities of the Council against the Catholic recusants thanks to the work of H. Aveling, *Post Reformation Catholicism in the East Riding* (East Yorkshire Local History Society, 1960), *Catholic Recusants of the West Riding* (Proc. Leeds Philosophical Society, Vol. X, 1963) and

Northern Catholics: the Catholic Recusants of the North Riding of York-shire (1966), and J. T. Cliffe, *Yorkshire Gentry from the Reformation to the Civil War* (London, 1966). D. M. Palliser in *The Reformation in York, 1534–53* (Borthwick Papers 40) has something to say about the Council and its activities in enforcing the Henrician settlement. R. B. Smith in *Land and Politics in the England of Henry VIII: the West Riding of Yorkshire, 1530–46* (Oxford, 1970) has chapters on the Pilgrimage of Grace and the suppression of the monasteries, but has little to say about the activity of the Council in the pacification of the north between 1537 and 1547. The Wentworth Woodhouse MSS now in Sheffield Public Library proved a disappointment to those who hoped that they would throw much more light on the working of the Council, and so did the discovery by the late Dr Purvis of the records of the High Commission for the Northern Province. These have been considered by P. Tyler *The Ecclesiastical Commission and Catholicism in the North* (Leeds, 1960) and in his article in *Northern History* (V, 1970), 'The Court of High Commission'. The local aspects and the relations of the Council with the city are covered in my *York and the Council of the North* (Borthwick Papers no. 5, 1954) and by A. G. Dickens and C. F. G. Forster in the chapters on Tudor and Stuart York in V.C.H. York City (London 1961). F. Drake's *Eboracum* (York, 1738) is rather disappointing as he had access to some of Widdrington's papers which may have included some of the missing records of the Council. He does print, in his appendices, the constitution of the suggested refoundation of the Council in 1665.

The careers of two of the Lords President have been the subject of special studies, Huntingdon by Dr Claire Cross in her *The Puritan Earl: the life of Henry Hastings, third Earl of Huntingdon 1536–1595* (London, 1967), and Strafford by Dr C. V. Wedgwood in *Strafford* (London, 1935, revised edition, 1968). The latter is enlightening on the intrigues which led to the appointment of Wentworth as Lord President. Miss Cross has also dealt more fully with one aspect of Huntingdon's work in 'The Earl of Huntingdon and the trial of Catholics in the North'. Recusant History, Vol. VIII, 1965).

PART SEVEN

The Close of the Tudor Age

THE CLOSE OF THE TUDOR AGE

by

JOEL HURSTFIELD

A historian who is not himself a literary critic is perhaps too
ready to see Shakespeare's plays as historical sources rather
than in terms of their form, plot, language, and imagery. He
may indeed be guilty of putting Shakespeare too much in his
time and too little in the context of the historical development
of English drama. Yet so handicapped, and perhaps also helped,
the historian does see in Shakespeare's work reflections of the
two societies in England or, to anticipate the phrase of Disraeli,
the two nations. If this conclusion is correct, and not merely
a subjective discovery in literature of what the historian finds
in Elizabethan and Jacobean society, then the plays – whether
histories or not – show over and over again the insecure grasp
of crown and government upon the authority they have inherited and claim. The crown which sits so uneasily on the
head of Henry IV is a burden to all Shakespeare's rulers. 'To
be a King and wear a crown,' said Elizabeth I to her Parliamentarians in 1601, 'is a thing more glorious to them that see
it, than it is pleasant to them that bear it.'[1] The force which
destroys Julius Caesar, Coriolanus, Richard II, Richard III is a
force which threatened the Tudor and Stuart monarchy. 'I am
Richard II,' said Elizabeth on another occasion to the historian
Lambarde, when referring to Shakespeare's play, 'know ye not
that?'[2]

For here was a monarchy which rested on two claims: that it
was of divine origin and that it governed by consent of the

whole people. These claims were not inherently contradictory since, in sixteenth-century political thought, representation did not imply election. The overwhelming majority of Englishmen in the time of Shakespeare did not possess the right to vote; and of those who had it, few ever had the opportunity to use it. Direct patronage, or agreement between factions, usually determined who should sit in Parliament. The basic assumption was that the leading men of the shire, however they were elected, spoke for their whole community; and this was not questioned until the middle of the seventeenth century when, in the tumult of revolution, a small minority called for a wider suffrage. But what was becoming a significant issue was whether the monarch made policy in the light only of divine guidance, or modified it where necessary on the advice of some 400 men gathered in the House of Commons and some sixty in the House of Lords. Was James I answerable for his policy in the next world only, as he believed, or could he be called to a reckoning in this?

It is often assumed that in Ulysses's plea for order and degree in *Troilus and Cressida* is an account of the Elizabethan form of social hierarchy as it existed. Yet what Ulysses is saying is that the Greek camp is sick because order and degree *no longer prevail*. In Shakespeare's England order and degree, where they existed at all, existed much more in form than substance; and so it had been throughout the sixteenth century. Indeed the real malaise was not because order and degree were in dissolution but because they were being imposed upon a society which had in many respects broken free from their rigidities. The tragedy of the Stuarts was that Charles I took degree, with monarchy at its apex, more seriously than had any of his predecessors, and far more seriously than would any of his Parliamentarians.

For Tudor society was fluid and pressing against the narrow channels into which church and state would confine it. To grasp this is fundamental to any understanding of Elizabethan or Jacobean society. It is not that the old order was dissolving. It was that a new more rigid order and degree were being imposed. It is not that the Tudor monarchy was fighting to retain its inherited powers, but it had enlarged these powers in a measure never enjoyed by its predecessors.

The central event which was to dominate the history of a whole century occurred a generation before Shakespeare's birth. In the 1530s Henry assumed on behalf of the monarchy powers which no other king of England had ever possessed. We call this event the English Reformation and the term is valid provided it is taken to describe a profound change in the constitution and society, perhaps more important than the religious change with which the term is associated.

Henry assumed the headship of the English church; and one uses the word assumed deliberately because the King did not derive his authority from Parliament – which did not possess the power to give it – but, as he stated, from God alone. Parliament was there simply to confirm, not grant this title, and to impose the penalties for disobedience. 'The King's Majesty,' says the Act of Supremacy of 1534, 'justly and rightfully is and oweth [ought] to be the supreme head.' The truth or otherwise of this statement could only be known when its author got to heaven; but in practice it became increasingly difficult for Henry VIII's successors to treat the whole religious settlement as if it were a private treaty between himself and the Almighty. The changes, first to Anglicanism under Henry VIII, then to radical Protestantism in the course of Edward VI's short reign, then sharply back to Catholicism during Mary's equally short reign, then back again to a moderate Protestant Anglicanism under Elizabeth I, had been too fundamental and too swift to permit a monarch to carry through by himself. Parliament came to see its own role, not simply as that of confirming the King's claims and executing his policy, but also as advising and commenting upon, criticizing and modifying the shape and content of the English church. It is the fashion to speak of a 'partnership' between Crown and Parliament in the Tudor period. By the end of Shakespeare's lifetime this 'partnership' resembled much more the unsettled relationship between one firm, the

Crown, which had overvalued its assets, and another, a more aggressive consortium, the Parliamentarians, which was thinking in terms of a take-over bid, so that it could run the business of government more efficiently and according to modern managerial techniques, in a new partnership.

When Shakespeare came to London much of this struggle lay in the future, but it was not very far away at the time that he left. What, however, we are seeing from Henry VIII's day onward is the emergence of the unitary, sovereign state, the state seeking supremacy in secular and spiritual things alike, and which was trying to reach into every crevice of men's thoughts and actions. Recognizing this process, More resigned his office of Lord Chancellor and then renounced life itself. We who can see the full-length Holbein portrait of Henry VIII with his legs astride, his gorgeous costume, his arrogant, beady eyes staring out on the world, see the visual image of the Leviathan state, sparing no man in its inexorable advance to power. Order and degree formed part of the new concept of the state, pressed on the nation by the Crown and its servants.

But below the flamboyant language of Henry VIII, the supreme head, the more modest language of Elizabeth I, and the renewed extravagance of James I, there was, in fact, an unstable and shifting balance of power. For though Parliament was, in the design of Henry VIII, no more than a ratifying and enforcing instrument for carrying through his revolution, the Parliamentarians were beginning to think otherwise. To understand the basis and framework of these advancing claims we must look beyond the court to the few million people who were Shakespeare's fellow countrymen.

It so happens that we have the work of two of Shakespeare's contemporaries to guide us in this. The first is Sir Thomas Smith, scholar, politician and diplomat, who wrote his *De Republica Anglorum* – only the title is in Latin – in 1565, the year after Shakespeare's birth. The second is Thomas Wilson, a minor figure in government circles, who wrote a survey of English society in about the year 1600, roughly halfway between the time of Shakespeare's arrival in London and his return to Stratford.

Smith wrote his book, which is enormously interesting as the only contemporary account of English government and society, while he was ambassador at the court of the Valois. He distrusted the French government and loathed the conditions of political and religious disorder which he saw all around him. By contrast, as he looked homeward, he saw indeed an ordered society secure in its internal peace, with each man acknowledging his appointed place in this happy commonwealth. (Even the criminals sentenced to death did not complain because they realized that the sentence had been lawfully given!)[3] Monarchy, aristocracy, gentry, burgesses, yeomen, all of them lived in settled, stable conditions, and performed duties appropriate to their rank. Smith even found a 'fourth sort of men which do not rule'[4]; and these, by the way, though he does not say so, were the overwhelming majority of the Queen's subjects. It is indeed, he argues, possible to identify each class by its very appearance: 'a gentleman (if he will be so accounted) must go like a gentleman, a yeoman like a yeoman, and a rascal like a rascal.'[5] But what is a gentleman? It is here that Smith lets reality break through the smooth surface of his two-dimensional survey. Gentlemen, he says, are being made 'good cheap' in England;[6] and the College of Heralds was always available to discover or invent an ancient lineage. Unkind critics, he acknowledges, scornfully call these *arrivistes* 'gentlemen of the first head'. Anyone, he says, who can afford to behave like a gentleman – 'who will bear the port, charge and countenance of a gentleman' – can soon be acknowledged as one.[7] Smith accepts that the *nouveaux riches* can make good their claim to gentility.

Thomas Wilson, writing about thirty-five years later, is less sure than is Smith about the ordered stability of England. Smith, of course, knows perfectly well that Tudor society is far more complex and indeterminate than his ordered hierarchy would imply. He gently tilts at the new families but assumes that they will rapidly adopt the postures of their class. Wilson's comments are not gently ironic but bitter. He was himself a younger son whose lot he laments, one of those, as he says, who inherit no more than 'that which the cat left on the malt heap'.[8] He is without land and without prospects. But he sees all around him the discouraging signs of an aggressive expansionist class from among whom he selects the upstart yeomen and lawyers for his most caustic comments.

The yeomen, he complains, 'must skip into his velvet breeches and silken doublet and, getting to be admitted into some Inn of Court or Chancery, must ever after think scorn to be called any other than gentleman.'[9] (It is good to be reminded of the somewhat different kind of yeomen from those to whom Shakespeare's Henry V and Richard III addressed their memorable words.) 'Prithee, nuncle,' asks the Fool of King Lear, 'tell me whether a madman be a gentleman or a yeoman' act 3, scene 6, ll. 9–13). To Lear's reply that the answer must be a king, the Fool retorts: No, a madman is 'a yeoman that has a gentleman to his son; for he's a mad yeoman that sees his son a gentleman before him'. Often these ambitions of the yeoman class are snuffed out in extravagance, but, says Wilson, the lawyers do better.

Many lawyers, says Wilson, are 'grown so great, so rich and so proud, that no other sort dare meddle with them'. The most eminent lawyers were, indeed, getting most of the profitable business, and the rest of the members of this overcrowded profession had to 'live by pettifogging'. So they pry into records and provoke litigation with the result that they 'undo the country people and buy up all the lands that are to be sold'. These parasites are to be found everywhere, except perhaps in the Isle of Anglesey 'which boast they never had lawyers nor foxes'[10]. It was, of course, not only the gentry who suffered. 'The first thing we do,' says Dick, the crony of Jack Cade, the rebel, 'let's kill all the lawyers' (2 Henry VI, act 4, scene 2, ll. 73–7). 'Nay that I mean to do,' replies Cade, 'Is not this a lamentable thing, that of the skin of an innocent lamb should be made parchment? That parchment, being scribbl'd o'er, should undo a man?'

Though England, of course, was not populated solely by lawyers, gentlemen and yeomen, we hear much of them in contemporary literature and politics because England was still essentially a rural country, and land the measure of a man's wealth and standing. Cloth, the only English industry of major importance, was still mainly a rural industry. But most men did not possess land, for example, the agricultural labourer, the textile worker in town and country, the retailer, the seaman, the schoolmaster, and many others. It is true that the enclosure movement, much of it for converting corn-land to sheep rearing, accompanied often by depopulation, had passed its peak by the time that Shakespeare was born; but its effects were still widely felt. Wealthy merchants and civil servants did own land for, as ever, the wealthy townsman sought to take root in the country. But, wherever they lived, they were alike acutely subject to the violent fluctuations of climate and harvest, of famine and plague, of commercial boom and slump, of war and peace.

During the whole of Shakespeare's lifetime there was not a single year when Europe was not engaged in war. England was not itself involved the whole time. From his birth until 1585 – roughly the time when he came to London – England was at peace, apart from isolated skirmishes. But for the rest of Elizabeth's reign, that is, for more than half the time he spent in London, she was at war, deeply committed, and at a prodigious cost, to a stubborn struggle in the Netherlands, in Ireland, and on the high seas. The new reign brought peace; but there could have been no period during Shakespeare's adult life when he would not see broken men returning from battle to which they had gone as volunteers or conscripts in defence of their own country, or as soldiers of fortune in foreign wars. 'What! a young knave and begging!' exclaims Falstaff. 'Is there not wars?' (2 *Henry IV*, act 1, scene 2, ll. 68–9). One should not be surprised that there are few plays of Shakespeare, whether history, comedy or tragedy, in which the sounds of war are not heard either on the stage or from the wings.

But far more widespread in their effects and implications were the threats of hunger and disease. The primitive state of English agriculture, and the inaccessibility of alternative supplies, meant that a wet summer and a ruined harvest brought high prices and hunger. Three wet summers in succession spelled out a major disaster as happened in the period 1594-6 and is best described in Titania's speech in *A Midsummer Night's Dream*. The price of corn, as compared with wages, has never been as high, before or since. London could sometimes import urgently needed corn via Danzig; other places using waterborne supplies might gain some relief. But inland transport, whether by water or land, was subject to all sorts of climatic hazards and was expensive for bulky commodities. Corn could double its price over relatively short distances.

Severe as these physical handicaps were, they were worsened by the sharp rise in population which extended for about a century after the 1530s. Probably the population doubled during this period, rising from about two and a half to five million, though the pace was uneven; and the population of London may have quadrupled, reaching a quarter of a million by the end of Shakespeare's life. Historians have not yet taken the measure or discovered the cause of this upward trend; but about its existence there is no doubt. Men like Hakluyt saw it clearly enough and used this evidence to urge emigration and colonial settlement. Again, the effects of this growth were intensified by the backward state of the economy. Industry had neither the capital, nor the markets, nor the raw materials, nor the technical resources to absorb this increased labour; nor had farmers the knowledge to force up production to meet the pressure of demand. Hence England faced the situation, familiar enough to us today in the West Indies and India, of a population outgrowing its industry and its subsistence, and forced therefore to leave. It gives us some insight into both Shakespeare's age and our own to reflect that England today, with some fifty million people is, in certain respects, under-populated while his England, with some five million, was threatened with overpopulation.

The other consequences of this are also familiar; unemployment, underemployment, and inflation. Underemployment, as we can see today in Spain, southern Italy and some of the emergent nations, was more widespread than unemployment. It is a condition in which men are not wholly without work, but work only part of the week or part of the day. In the earlier centuries this was in some respects masked by two characteristics of medieval life: a part of the population was taken out of the labour market into monasteries and nunneries; and secondly, the large number of saints' days in any case reduced the length of the working week. When Protestant England abolished monasteries and nunneries and drastically reduced the saints' days, the implicit conditions of under-employment became explicit.

But even more widespread were the effects of inflation. This, as always, affected the whole population. But it did not affect the whole population in the same way. It is a common enough phenomenon, in any time of inflation, that some of the rich grow richer and some of the poor grow poorer. So it was in Tudor England. Fortune, says Henry IV

> '... either gives a stomach and no food –
> Such are the poor, in health – or else a feast,
> And takes away the stomach – such are the rich ...'
> (2 *Henry IV*, act 4, scene 4, ll. 105–7)

Many lost, for example, tenants (including copyholders) whose legal insecurity of tenure, or sheer weakness, made it possible to evict them; those landlords who found no means of raising rents to meet a changed situation, or had to bankrupt themselves to meet the heavy cost of litigation, or even dowries for a string of daughters; artisans whose labour was more plentiful than the food they ate; and the Crown whose income simply could not be enlarged to meet the increased cost of living, administration, diplomacy, and war. Who gained? Many merchants who sold on a rising market; those landlords who could force rents up and generally modernize their estates; many lawyers whose services are always needed in time of rapid change. All the evidence points to the increasing importance of these classes in society. We ask, therefore, what was their role in government?

The provincial gentry supplied the justices of the peace and the sheriffs. They served as amateurs but many of them had spent a year or more at either Oxford or Cambridge, or at the Inns of Court in London, the third university of England. They had both judicial and administrative duties, including the maintenance of order, the supervision of roads and bridges, the apprenticing of poor children, the fixing of wages, and the organization of poor relief. A proportion of them worked hard and conscientiously but others were slack and easily responded to favour or gifts. They were not as bad as Shallow and Silence but some were probably not much better. The provincial administration for military affairs was no better. Under a leading nobleman as lord lieutenant it was factious, sometimes corrupt and thoroughly amateur.

Any study of Tudor provincial administration displays the great gap between the claims and the powers of the Crown. Its writ ran only as far as the gentry cared to obey it. Behind the writ lay the threat; and a summons to appear before the Star Chamber in London was not lightheartedly received by justices who corrupted administration or juries who falsified verdicts. Many a great person in his shire was cut down to size by the government in London. But there were limits to the amount that it could do against the pressures of vested interests or just simply idleness or stupidity in the shire. Hence it is nowadays said by many historians that this was not an autocracy and that 'Tudor despotism' is a nineteenth-century myth.

Yet this ignores one important element in government power: its control over communication. If the printing press in one sense weakens central authority because it makes possible the dissemination of minority opinions, in another it comes to its aid. Certainly, the government used pamphlets and homilies, addresses by high court judges at the assizes, sermons, proclamations, preambles to statutes to expound and popularize its aims to all who could read, write, or listen. And the royal progress provided a dazzling, theatrical cavalcade through the towns and villages of southern England – these costly, elaborate processions never got to the north – and helped to implant in the popular imagination the divine attributes of the sovereign. Meanwhile, on the negative side, the strong censorship exercised over all forms of literature, secular no less than divine, did much to uphold the sacred virtues of the established order. The penalties for dissent were heavy and they grew heavier in the generation after Shakespeare's death as the fundamental dispute within the nation intensified and the country drifted into civil war. The dispute centred upon the nature of authority, and it dominates many of his plays.

The Tudor Crown under Henry VIII had absorbed too much power over church and state, over thought and action. Divinity might hedge a king – if there were also arms to defend him; but it could not shield him from the doubts of his critics, or provide him with the necessary funds to govern. By the end of the sixteenth century, even the relatively austere Elizabeth was being forced to sell land to meet the exhausting costs of war. The more she lived on capital, the more she and her successors would have to call on parliamentary support. But it was the same kind of men who were influential in the shires who were also influential in Parliament, and Parliament was unwilling to grant money without a direct influence on government policy. Yet this control no monarch of the day was willing to accept, least of all the goddess Elizabeth or the kingly Solomon, James I. Hence the conditions of deadlock which were developing during Shakespeare's last decade in London. The anointed king held the spiritual and constitutional titles and the authority to determine policy, without the economic power to carry it through. The Commons possessed the economic power without the constitutional right to make policy.

'The state of monarchy', James I once told his faithful Parliamentarians, 'is the supremest thing upon earth. For kings are not only God's lieutenants upon earth and sit upon God's throne, but even by God himself they are called Gods.'[11] These Parliamentarians were many of them astute, experienced men of the world who were hearing one thing and seeing another. They looked upon this man, ungainly, undignified, impoverished. They saw a patronage system which under Elizabeth, in spite of her mistakes, was usually used skilfully to distribute power and to bring the ablest men to the top. They had seen the whole system shudder at the end of the reign when the Earl of Essex had declined to submit to the controls essential to monarchical rule. The Essex rebellion, in which the Earl of Southampton, Shakespeare's patron, was involved, had it succeeded, would have put the clock back to the Wars of the Roses. Elizabeth regained control; and royal patronage remained the only viable system of government between the decline of medieval feudalism and the rise of modern party government. But James never grasped its full purpose. To him the criteria for the elevation of his public servants were not their wisdom and statecraft but their physical charms and his personal affection. The monarch who declared that kings were called gods by God himself could thus write to his favourite, the Earl of Somerset: 'Do not all courtesies and places come through your office as Chamberlain, and rewards through your father-in-law as Treasurer. Do not you two as it were hedge in all the court with a manner of necessity to depend upon you?'[12] Patronage was debased into favouritism; and it was there for all men to see. Was divinity enough to hedge a king?

Decay and division spread out from the court to the upper ranks of society and on through the shires. So, too, contempt and resistance began to find voice among those who had always measured monarchy against the divine criteria of the Bible. For Puritanism was now a force to be reckoned with.

When it first emerged under that name, early in Elizabeth's reign, the term was applied to a minority of churchmen, Members of Parliament and others who felt that the Anglican Reformation had stopped short of its goal. It had not established anything resembling a biblical commonwealth, now developing in Geneva, nor had it purged the English church of Romish rituals and organization. Some of the leaders of Puritanism were to be found in the upper ranks of church and state, and among the *jeunesse dorée* of the age, of which the best example was the Earl of Essex. Some of these political leaders had a deep and fervent interest in religion, as had the Earl of Huntingdon, others saw it much more as part of a political alignment. Many M.P.s saw it also as a great force for resisting the alien power of Spain, and the alien influence represented by Mary, Queen of Scots.

From our point of view, however, a new and important element became apparent, late in the reign, in the shape of moral puritanism and, more especially, sabbatarianism. Since Puritans used the Bible as a guide to conduct, not simply to faith but to political and social life, and since they could read it in their own language, it took on for them a greater importance than it had ever held. They made a serious attempt to recreate some of the conditions and standards of behaviour which had been adopted by the biblical Children of Israel. Part of this was the Mosaic injunction to remember the Sabbath day and keep it holy. In 1595 the publication of Nicholas Bownd's *Doctrine of the Sabbath* gave formal exposition to this developing theme; but this was only part, albeit an important part, of the increasingly rigid moral stance assumed by the Puritans. The long struggle between the Puritans and the theatre had begun. To be virtuous was to renounce cakes and ale. The controversy over sabbatarianism was bitterly fought for decades with the result, said Thomas Fuller, that 'the sabbath itself had no rest'[13]. Puritan dissent challenged the fundamentals of church, state, and society.

Catholic dissent was less dangerous though the government

was bound to take it seriously in the light of the whole European situation of national and civil war. Catholicism in England, it is true, collected its own extremists who played dangerous political games with foreign powers, but they were a tiny minority. The Crown for its part tried to stamp out Catholicism by increasingly severe penalties. Yet in spite of this, the overwhelming majority of the Catholics remained loyal subjects of the Crown in the time of its danger, as during the threat of the Spanish Armada in 1588, and Gunpowder Plot in 1605. Only in Ireland, where Catholicism formed part of a domestic desire for self-expression and independence, did it become a truly hostile movement. But in England Puritanism was more of a threat than Catholicism, partly because the Puritans functioned *within* the governing class, and partly because their whole philosophy found its source and authority, not in monarchy and hierarchy, but in a quasi-egalitarian biblical commonwealth.

Here then was evidence that the elaborate, gilded superstructure of a divine royal order rested insecurely on its religious foundations. And when the House of Commons became the sounding board for religious criticism and political discontent, as it did during the last years of Shakespeare's life, the whole system was under severe strain. Yet it would be wrong to paint these later years of Shakespeare's life in sombre colours. For the growing intensity of the debate was itself a sign of the intellectual vigour, independence, and adventurousness distributed widely within the nation.

It was a time, too, of the growth of a social conscience. In the early sixteenth century Hythlodaye in More's *Utopia* could write bitterly: 'When I consider and weigh in my mind all these commonwealths which nowadays anywhere do flourish, so God help me, I can perceive nothing but a certain conspiracy of rich men procuring their own commodities under the name and title of the commonwealth.'[14] There was still the division between the two nations; and Smith's 'Fourth sort of men which do not rule' lived often in dire poverty at the edge of starvation. Yet Elizabeth's reign had seen the emergence of imaginative policies for social welfare, and the formulation of good machinery for carrying them through. There was at last the open recognition that innocent and hardworking men could be caught up in the harsh consequences of an economic slump. It was now acknowledged that somehow work must be found or relief given. The state too, in the shape of the county or town, was assuming some degree of responsibility for the orphan, the sick, and the aged. Unevenly, pragmatically, the governing classes saw that their own strength and the survival of their society were bound up with the recognition of social responsibility for their fellow Englishmen. One unforeseen result of this was that the civil war of the seventeenth century was not a social revolution as well.

London had been a pioneer in welfare matters, as in so much else. And here in the capital, in the years when Shakespeare was turning his thoughts towards London, was gathered the greatest talent in politics, law and administration. Here were the palace, its law courts, Parliament, the city gilds and companies; here was diversity, a teeming thrusting population, a questing interest in novelty. Here were poets, churchmen, politicians, lawyers, pamphleteers. Here was money seeking an outlet in commerce, piracy and the gentler arts of peace. Never before in English history had there been such a concentration of wealth, talent and opportunity. Here, then, was a 'wide and universal theatre' embracing the whole capital, with an audience in their places waiting for the play to start.

NOTES

1. J. E. Neale, *Elizabeth I and her Parliaments* (1957), II, 391.
2. J. E. Neale, *Elizabeth I* (1934), p. 381.
3. Thomas Smith, *De Republica Anglorum*, ed. L. Alston (Cambridge, 1906), p. 106.
4. *Ibid.*, p. 46.
5. *Ibid.*, p. 41.
6. *Ibid.*, p. 39.
7. *Ibid.*, p. 40. Cf. W. Harrison, *Description of England* (1577) upon which Smith almost certainly drew.

8. Thomas Wilson, *The State of England Anno Domini 1600*, ed. F. J. Fisher, *Camden Miscellany*, 1936, XVI, 24.

9. *Ibid.*, p. 19.

10. *Ibid.*, p. 24-5.

11. D. H. Willson, *King James VI and I* (1956), p. 243.

12. *Ibid.*, p. 350.

13. Cited in P. Collinson: 'The Beginnings of English Sabbatarianism', *Studies in Church History*, I, 221.

14. Thomas More, *Utopia*, ed. J. R. Lumby (Cambridge, 1885), p. 162. I am using the Tudor translation not the modern one.

ACKNOWLEDGEMENT

Reprinted from *A New Companion to Shakespearian Studies*, ed. K. Muir and S. Schoenbaum, Cambridge, 1971, pp. 168–79, by kind permission of the syndics of the Cambridge University Press.

INDEX